— WALKER'S COMPANION —

SCOTLAND

WALKER'S COMPANION
SCOTLAND

HAMISH BROWN, RENNIE McOWAN & RICHARD MEARNS

Photography by John Heseltine
With an Introduction by JIMMIE MacGREGOR

TED SMART

This edition produced for
The Book People Ltd,
Hall Wood Avenue,
Haydock,
St Helens WA11 9UL

First published in 1994 by Ward Lock

Printed and bound in Spain by Graficromo S.A.,Cordoba

ISBN 0-7063-7245-X

CONTENTS

INTRODUCTION

As a boy, the highest place in my world was the flagpole mound in Glasgow's Springburn park, and the wildest places I knew were the streets of the city. My secret hidden places were the stair wells, dunnies and back courts of the tenements, and my cliffs were four stories of sandstone. Springburn stands high in Glasgow, and from the viewpoint of the park there were grand, and seemingly remote vistas to the north. Between the canyons of the high buildings which packaged the poor, there were glimpses of another bigger and emptier world. A world of blurred blue hills, and mysteriously, glints of snow in spring sunshine. As I grew, I was drawn to these places. The hills were the Campsies, a mere 11 miles distant, and the unseasonal snow gleamed on Ben Lomond at only twice that distance. The bicycle made the Campsies accessible, and a great physical day began with the cycle ride to Campsie Glen. The bike would then be hidden, so that I could climb to the summit ridge and wander miles of open moor, tracking down the nests of peewit, curlew and wheatear. Once, on the loose rock, there was the thrill of a kestrel's nest with five russet eggs. On descending from the hill, one could cool off in the icy waters that ran through the glen before pedalling home. Through walking, cycling and cross-country running, (we hadn't heard of jogging) I became familiar with the countryside around where I then lived, on the edge of the town. I was fascinated by the wildlife, and the more I learned, the more I wanted to know.

I was moving farther afield now, and in my teenage years I was already familiar with what is now known as the West Highland Way. I discovered the Scottish Youth Hostels, and made good use of all those close to Glasgow, as well as some further afield: Fintry, Inverbeg, Crianlarich, Glencoe, The Isle of Arran, (a favourite place) Rowerdennan, Ardgarten and Auchendennan. Later, when a student, I worked at Auchendennan as an assistant warden; and much later as an art teacher, I introduced scores of youngsters to the outdoors by walking them over the hills from Campsie Glen to Fintry Youth Hostel.

When I became embroiled in the world of folk music, skiffle

and jazz in London, the outdoors played a diminished part in my life for some years, although Hampstead Heath was always there for walking and running, and concert tours abroad provided some off-beat opportunities, like blistering hill walks in Israel. When touring in Scotland's highlands and islands, I found it useful to have a pair of boots in the car, for there were opportunities for walks between concert venues. I still remember the thrill of finding my first ring ouzel's nest, on a little walk on stolen time between Brora and Inverness.

The direction of my life and career has changed once again, and I now find myself privileged to be making radio and television programmes all over Scotland, and it is strange to reflect that all my youthful obsessions which were considered odd, if not downright eccentric, have now become common-place. Any library or good bookshop now has a section devoted to outdoor pursuits, and manufacturers of boots, outdoor clothing and climbing gear emerge from their Porsches wearing beatific smiles.

The increase in the number of people taking to the hills and wild places carries its own dangers of course, but on balance, it can only be a good thing that more and more people are enjoying Scotland's countryside and wilderness areas, and, most importantly, caring for them. *Walker's Companion: Scotland* can only add to the interest in, and concern for, the country. The three authors of this book are all vastly experienced outdoor people, who combine knowledge with real concern for what has shaped Scotland's landscape and country life in the past, what is happening now, and what could take place in the future.

Rennie McOwan's name is known to anyone interested in Scotland, and in addition to his numerous writings, he does regular broadcasts, and has even helped me out on my own radio and television programmes. Despite the fact that Rennie deplores the concept of marked walk-ways, and I make programmes about them, we remain friends, and I have a deep respect for his knowledge of Scottish life, including history, ornithology and the arts. Although Rennie McOwan is a very busy writer, lecturer and broadcaster, he still spends as much time as possible on the hills, and is descended from a long line of outdoor people. His grandfather and great-grandfather were well-known stalkers on the Langwell and Braemore estate in Caithness, and feature prominently in the memoirs of the Laird, the Duke of Portland.

Hamish Brown is one of Scotland's best-known outdoor men, with eleven books and countless newspaper and magazine articles to his credit. He shares Rennie McOwan's interest in ornithology, music and the arts, and while he is very much associated with Scotland, he was brought up in the Far East, and has travelled extensively in places as diverse as Morocco, Ethiopia, Iceland, Poland, Corsica and the Pyrenees.

Richard Mearns has made a special study of the lives of early Scottish ornithologists, and like our other two authors, has travelled widely. Richard is employed as a senior countryside ranger on the western section of the Southern Upland Way, and is especially attracted to walks in the south of Scotland. In addition to his other writings, he has undertaken scientific publications on the raven and the peregrine falcon.

In *Walker's Companion: Scotland*, our three writers have given us a huge range and variety of routes, together with enough densely textured background information to keep most outdoor enthusiasts interested and challenged for a long time to come. Interesting as they may all be to read, their common object is to persuade you to lace up your boots and venture forth to find out about this wonderful country for yourself.

Jimmie Macgregor

INTRODUCTION TO THE ROUTE DESCRIPTIONS

1. ACCESS

See pages 123–4.

2. ASCENT

The amount of climbing involved in each route has been estimated from the Outdoor Leisure or 1:50 000 maps as appropriate and should be regarded as approximate only.

3. CAR-PARKS

The nearest public car-park is given. There will be many places where a car can be parked by the wayside, but it must be done with care, as indiscriminate parking can be a great nuisance to local people.

4. INTERESTING FEATURES

The best position for seeing these is indicated both in the route descriptions and on the maps by *(1)*, *(2)*, etc.

5. LENGTH

These are strictly 'map miles' estimated from the Outdoor Leisure or 1:50 000 maps; no attempt has been made to take into account any ascent or descent involved.

6. MAPS

The maps are drawn to a scale of approximately 1:25 000 or 1:50 000 and all names are as given on Ordnance Survey maps. Field boundaries in particular, which can be a mixture of hedge, fence and wall, should be taken as a 'best description'. The maps have in the main been drawn so that the route goes from the bottom to the top of a page. This will enable the reader to 'line up' the map in the direction walked whilst still holding the book in the normal reading position. The arrow on each map points to grid north. The scale of some small features has been slightly exaggerated for clarity. For easy cross-reference, the relevant Outdoor Leisure and Landranger sheets are indicated on each map.

7. ROUTE DESCRIPTION

The letters 'L' and 'R' stand for left and right respectively. Where these are used for changes of direction then they imply a turn of about 90° when facing in the direction of the walk. 'Half L' and 'half R' indicate a half-turn, i.e. approximately 45°, and 'back half L' or 'back half R' indicate three-quarter turns, i.e.

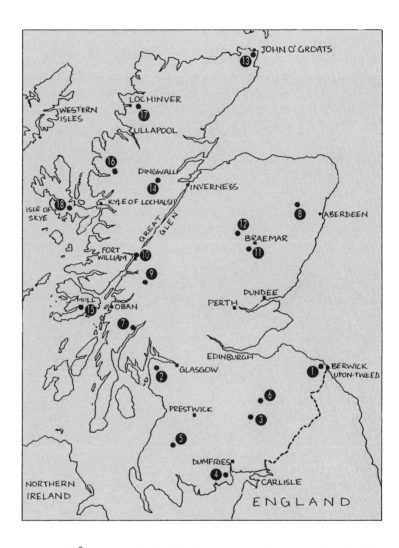

FIGURE 1
The approximate starting points of the walks

about 135°. PFS stands for 'Public Footpath Sign', PBS for 'Public Bridleway Sign' and OS for 'Ordnance Survey'.

To avoid constant repetition, it should be assumed that all stiles and gates mentioned in the route description are to be crossed (unless there is a specific statement to the contrary).

8. STANDARD OF THE ROUTES

The briefest examination of the route descriptions that follow will show that the routes described cover an enormous range of both length and difficulty; the easiest can probably be undertaken by a family party at almost any time of the year whilst the hardest are only really suitable for experienced walkers who are both fit and well-equipped. Any walker therefore who is contemplating following a route should make

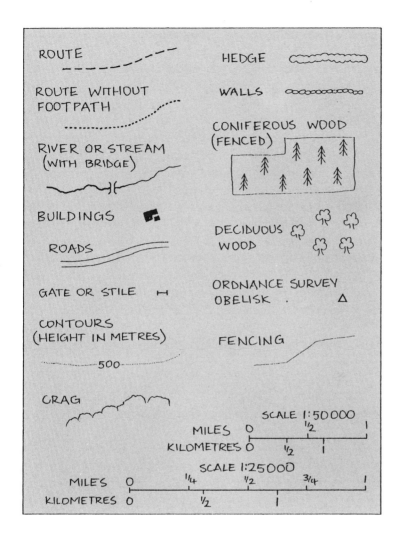

FIGURE 2 *Symbols used on detailed route maps*

sure before starting that it is within his or her ability.

It is not easy in practice, however, to give an accurate picture of the difficulty of any route, because it is dependent upon a number of factors and will in any case vary considerably from day to day with the weather. Any consideration of weather conditions must, of course, be left to the walker himself (but read the section on safety first). Apart from that, it is probably best to attempt an overall assessment of difficulty based upon the length, amount of ascent and descent, problems of route-finding and finally, upon the roughness of the terrain.

Each of the routes has therefore been given a grading based upon a consideration of these factors and represented by the bold numerals which precede each walk title. A general description of each grade follows:

Easy (1) Generally short walks (up to about 7 miles, 11 km) over well-defined paths, with no problems of route-finding. Some climbing may be involved, but mostly over fairly gradual slopes with only short sections of more difficult ground.

Moderate (2) Rather longer walks (up to about 9 miles, 14 km), mostly over paths, but with sections where route-finding will be more difficult. Mountain summits may be reached with climbing over steeper and rougher ground.

More strenuous (3) Generally longer walks (7–16 miles, 11–26 km), with prolonged spells of climbing. Some rough ground calling for good route-finding ability, perhaps with stretches of scrambling.

Very strenuous (4) Only for the few, involving long distances (over 16 miles, 26 km), with a considerable amount of climbing.

The walks are arranged in order of increasing difficulty within each section.

A summary of each walk is given at the head of each section with information on length, amount of climbing and any special difficulties, such as scrambling, that will be met along the way.

9. STARTING AND FINISHING POINTS
Unless it is stated otherwise, the location of each starting point is given by the number of the appropriate Landranger (1:50 000) map with a six-figure grid reference (see page 126); thus (78-874128) indicates grid reference 874128 which can be found on Landranger sheet no. 78.

10. TIME FOR COMPLETION
The usual method of estimating the length of time needed for a walk is by Naismith's Rule: 'For ordinary walking allow one hour for every 3 miles (5 km) and add one hour for every 2000 feet (600 m) of ascent; for backpacking with a heavy load allow one hour for every 2½ miles (4 km) and one hour for every 1500 feet (450 m) of ascent.' However, for many this tends to be over-optimistic and it is better for each walker to form an assessment of his or her own performance over one or two walks. Naismith's Rule also makes no allowance for rest or food stops or for the influence of weather conditions.

SELECTED WALKS IN THE SOUTHERN UPLANDS

Richard Mearns

Signpost along the Southern Upland Way

INTRODUCTION

Although chosen for the variety of scenery, length and geographical position, these six walks reflect my involvement with southern Scotland over the last twenty years. As a student in Edinburgh I often escaped to Holyrood Park in those days when I lacked a car, St Abb's Head was an exciting prospect, and it remains so for anyone remotely interested in birds. In the summer months the cliffs are thronged with thousands upon thousands of sea-birds.

In 1974, when I moved to Dumfries to begin a nine-year study of peregrines, I had to range all over southern Scotland to the highest and most isolated hills as well as to the long, convoluted coastline—in fact, anywhere there could be nesting cliffs. Each breeding season my travels recommenced, but the first two years were undoubtedly the best because everything then was fresh and exciting. How I wish I had known the landscape before foreign conifers began to dominate the upland areas and change the character of Galloway so severely. However, much that is good remains and I could still have chosen from any number of hill routes. In the end, I have settled on two old favourites, the Merrick and the Grey Mare's Tail. These walks provide splendid introductions to the treeless parts of the Galloway and Moffat hills respectively.

One winter in the 1970s as I waited for spring I studied the roosting and feeding behaviour of the waders on the north Solway shore. It can, of course, be dangerous to wander out across the mudflats but the splendour of the Solway can still be appreciated by climbing Criffel on a clear day to watch the incoming tide surging in over the mud and swirling up the channels and creeks.

When I became the Ranger for the western section of the Southern Upland Way my many years of hill walking meant that I already knew much of the country through which it passes. One of my walks incorporates a tiny portion of this wonderful 212 mile (340 km) coast-to-coast long-distance footpath. In the Borders Region, it makes use of the Minchmoor Road, an ancient trackway which has become a favourite stretch for all

Southern Upland Way walkers.

Rocks near St Abb's Head

The last walk that I have selected lies just outside my wife's home town of Greenock. The Greenock Cut once supplied water and power to the town; the path beside it now provides an unusual low gradient route suitable for family parties. In the 1820s the walks around the town were described as being among the finest in Europe. Since then Greenock has expanded, not always very attractively, but this is still a fine walk with much of interest and with many outstanding views. Northwards beyond the Clyde the peaks of Ben Lomond and Ben Vorlich give a hint of the type of walking that is available elsewhere in the country.

1·1

St Abb's Head

STARTING AND
FINISHING POINT
Northfield Farm
Visitor centre (67-
913674). On the
B6438 between
Coldingham and
St Abb's.

LENGTH
3½ miles (5.5 km)

ASCENT
400 ft (120 m).

These awesome cliffs rise up nearly 300 ft (90 m) above the
North Sea, and hold one of the largest concentrations of
breeding sea-birds on the east coast of mainland Britain. The
best time to see the birds is in spring and early summer, but this
easy walk is dramatic at all times of year.

ROUTE DESCRIPTION (Map 1)

The first part of the walk is clearly waymarked. From the Visitor
Centre (1) continue downhill to a stile beside the B6438. Turn
half L across the farm entrance to a gap in the wall where four
steps lead down to the start of a fenced path which runs parallel
with the road. Turn L after 250 yards (225 m) when the path
meets a high wall with an information board. After passing
through two kissing-gates the first good views of the red
sandstone seacliffs begin to unfold and the air can be filled with
the sight, sound and smell of sea-birds (2). Continue along the
cliff-top path, remembering to look back from time to time
towards the village and harbour of St Abbs (3), and the cliffs
leading southwards to Eyemouth.

At Horsecastle Bay there is a stile. Turn L along the upper
side of the fence to the outside corner of the field where the
closely cropped grassy path becomes indistinct. Turn half R up
the gully bottom which leads to the cliff edge again, keeping an
eye out in summer for the flowers of the common rock rose.

Join the metalled road at the lighthouse (4) and follow it
down towards Pettico Wick. On rounding the first sharp bend,
you will have a sudden view of flat-topped cliffs stretching away
northwards to Fast Castle and beyond. In the distance the Bass
Rock rises precipitously from the Firth of Forth, and on clear
days the low flat Isle of May can be seen further eastwards, with
the Kingdom of Fife beyond.

At the lowest point in the road, turn L and follow the narrow
path down the L (eastern) side of the Mire Loch (5). Carry on
beyond the dam to the fence and turn L along it to rejoin the
path which leads back to the car-park.

Pettico Wick

1 *Visitor Centre*

St Abb's Head National Nature Reserve was purchased in 1980 by the National Trust for Scotland, which administers it as a wildlife reserve in conjunction with the Scottish Wildlife Trust. Jointly, they provide a Ranger service. The newly created Visitor Centre offers information on the fauna and flora of the area, including taped sea-bird noises.

2 *Sea-birds*

The towering cliffs offer nesting ledges to a host of sea-birds, the most numerous being guillemots and kittiwakes, each of which species numbers in excess of 10,000 pairs. There are

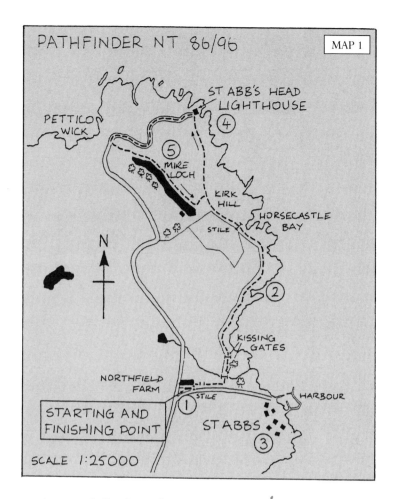

PATHFINDER NT 86/96   MAP 1

ST ABB'S HEAD LIGHTHOUSE ④

PETTICO WICK

⑤ MIRE LOCH

KIRK HILL

HORSECASTLE BAY

STILE

N

②

KISSING GATES

NORTHFIELD FARM

STILE

HARBOUR

STARTING AND FINISHING POINT ①

ST ABBS ③

SCALE 1:25000

also razorbills, shags, fulmars, herring gulls and a few puffins. Gannets do not breed here but thousands pass offshore, to and from the Bass Rock.

3 *St Abbs*

The village is named after St Aebba who founded a church here in the seventh century. The present church and harbour were built by a member of the brewing family of Usher who stipulated, despite his business, that there should be no public house here—and the village still lacks one.

4 *St Abb's Head Lighthouse*

The light was built in 1862 to help safeguard shipping on this storm-battered coast. But so great was the gale of 14 October 1881 that half the fishing fleet of Eyemouth (24 boats) sank, with the loss of 129 lives.

5 *The Mire Loch*

This artificial loch was constructed in 1901 for trout fishing. Gulls, coots, mallards, goldeneyes and tufted ducks may be seen here in the autumn and winter, if the water does not freeze.

Opposite *The harbour at St Abb's*

1·2

THE GREENOCK CUT

STARTING AND
FINISHING
POINT
Cornalees Bridge
Visitor Centre (63-
246722). Turn east
off the A742
Greenock-Inverkip
road to Loch
Thom.

LENGTH
7½ miles (12 km)

ASCENT
300 ft (90 m)

This easy circular walk follows an old aqueduct from the
Cornalees Bridge Visitor Centre to the outskirts of Greenock
and returns over the moors past Loch Thom. There are
interesting views northwards across the Firth of Clyde and
south-westwards to Arran and Bute.

ROUTE DESCRIPTION (Map 2)

From the car-park at the Visitor Centre *(1)* follow the signs to
the nature trail by turning R and then immediately L across the
old Cornalees Bridge. Go through a metal gate on the R and
down the concrete steps to the sluice-gates. The far one, with
the wooden walkway, used to help control the water levels in
the Greenock Cut *(2)*. Pass to the L of it and follow the narrow
aqueduct for the next 5½ miles (9 km), always keeping it on
your R. There are a number of metal kissing-gates along the
route, but the way is always obvious. The first gate is reached
after ¼ mile (400 m), and 20 yards (18 m) beyond it the nature
trail forks off to the L across a stile. By following the Cut you
will soon come to Shielhill Farm *(3)*, where there are two gates
on opposite sides of the metalled road. Once clear of the first
field and a short wooded section, you will have views on the L of
Arran, Bute and the outer Clyde.

Along the Cut there are several navvies' stone huts *(4)* which
date from the time that the channel was cut. The path seems to
follow the same contour but in fact drops gradually downhill all
the way to Overton Long Dam, where a road crosses the Cut
beside a cottage. Turn R across the bridge and go through yet
another metal kissing-gate. The rough track skirts the edges of
two small reservoirs before climbing gently uphill. Looking
back, there are views of the urban sprawl of Greenock, its
redundant shipyard cranes, the Clyde and distant Ben Lomond.
The large, prominent, dark-brick building is the Inverclyde
Royal Hospital. One feature not shown on your map is an
elliptical 'sandbank' lying between Greenock and Helensburgh.

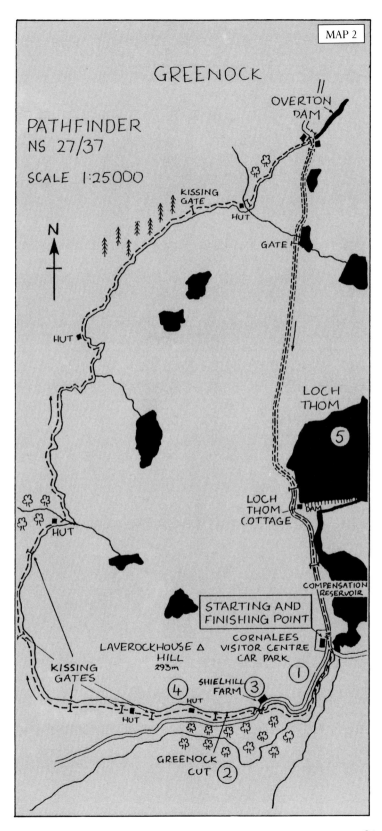

MAP 2

GREENOCK

PATHFINDER
NS 27/37

SCALE 1:25000

N

OVERTON DAM

KISSING GATE

HUT

GATE

HUT

LOCH THOM

5

LOCH THOM COTTAGE

DAM

HUT

COMPENSATION RESERVOIR

STARTING AND FINISHING POINT

CORNALEES VISITOR CENTRE CAR PARK

1

LAVEROCKHOUSE △ HILL 293m

SHIELHILL FARM

3

4

HUT

KISSING GATES

HUT

GREENOCK CUT

2

21

This is the upturned, rusting hull of a Greek sugar ship which capsized in 1974.

A mile (1.6 km) from Overton, Loch Thom (5) and the smaller Compensation Reservoir come into view. From Loch Thom Cottage the road leads directly back to the car-park.

1 *Cornalees Bridge Visitor Centre*
   The site of the new Visitor Centre is part of the 35,000-acre (14,165 hectares) Clyde-Muirshiel Regional Park. There is a Ranger Service and a signposted circular nature trail down the wooded Shielhill Glen. The lower section of the glen is now a Site of Special Scientific Interest, yet until 160 years ago it was an active quarry which supplied the sandstone for many of Greenock's buildings.

2 *Greenock Cut*
   Foreign shipping, the lack of a sewerage system and a severely inadequate water supply combined to make Greenock the unhealthiest town in Scotland in the nineteenth century. The town was expanding rapidly and the demand for fresh water increased, so the Greenock Cut was devised to alleviate some of the town's problems. From 1827, the aqueduct supplied fresh water and also provided water power to as many as twenty-six factories on the eastern fall-line from Overton Long Dam. In sharp contrast to the Cut, which only drops 27 ft (8 m) in 5½ miles (9 km), the fall-line drops 512 ft (156 m) between Overton and the Clyde.

3 *Shielhill Farm*
   The Ranger Service occasionally takes parties down to the farm so that they can watch, from a special viewing platform, the cows being milked.

4 *Navvies' huts*
   The Shaws Water Joint Stock Company guaranteed a flow of 1200 cubic ft (33,980 l) of water per minute for twelve hours a day down the eastern fall-line. Navvies used the stone shelters, especially during the difficult task of winter maintenance as they struggled to keep the channel free of snow and ice.

5 *Loch Thom*
   Originally known as the Little Caspian, the loch was renamed to commemorate Robert Thom who had the vision to bring the water around Dunrod Hill to Greenock. In 1971 a 1¼-mile (2 km) tunnel linked the reservoir with the town and Thom's Greenock Cut became obsolete after 144 years of use. It is now a scheduled Ancient Monument.

Opposite Looking towards Loch Thom Cottage

GREY MARE'S TAIL AND LOCH SKEEN

STARTING AND
FINISHING
POINT
National Trust for
Scotland car-park
(79-186145). 5
miles (8 km) south-
west of St Mary's
Loch on the A708
Moffat-Selkirk
road.

LENGTH
6 miles (9.5 km)

ASCENT
1900 ft (580 m)

Impressive views of the Grey Mare's Tail waterfall, an isolated hill loch and the surrounding craggy hills, combine to make this walk the scenic rival of many a route in the western Highlands. Owned by the National Trust for Scotland, it provides an excellent introduction to the Moffat hills where open moorland is still predominantly managed for sheep.

ROUTE DESCRIPTION (Map 3)

From the information shelter beside the walled car-park, two paths are clearly visible. One leads only to the base of the Grey Mare's Tail *(1)*. The other, which cuts diagonally across the hillside to the north, is the route to be taken for Loch Skeen. Cross the Tail Burn by the road bridge, turn half L and head up the steps to an old sheep enclosure where information boards explain the local geology and Charles Lapworth's interest in it *(2)*. The path from here to the loch is obvious and easy to follow, but do not stray from it in an attempt to get a better look at the falls: the grassy slopes are slippery and have claimed a number of lives.

The majority of visitors to Loch Skeen *(3)* stop at the water's edge and if it is misty on the higher ground it is advisable that you also turn back here. But on good days the high circuit around the loch is well worthwhile and can be very dramatic.

To climb higher, turn L over the makeshift ford beside the loch, skirt around the lower end of the loch and head north-west towards the prominent conical hill ahead. Follow the faint zig-zag path up it, keeping well away from the precipices of Mid Craig on the R. At the summit follow magnetic bearing 295° for 750 yards (700 m) to meet a fence, with a ruined wall behind. Turn R and follow the fence to Firthybrigg Head, then down to Talla Nick and up again to the plateau of Lochcraig Head (2625 ft, 800 m). From here there are excellent views down to Loch Skeen. To the west, north and east are the Lowther, Moorfoot and Eildon Hills respectively.

Opposite Waterfall
on the Tail Burn

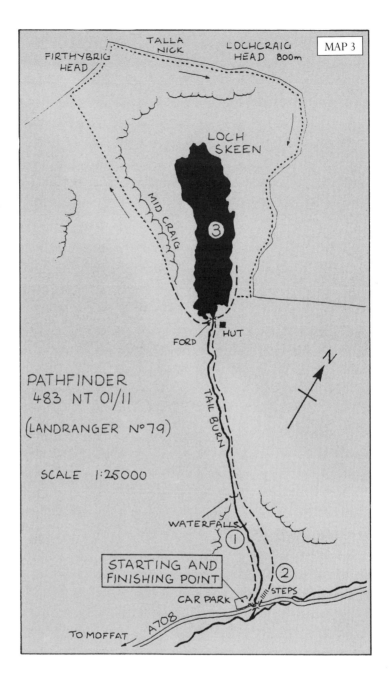

To return, continue to follow the same fence as it leads steeply downhill. On the more level ground east of the loch carefully negotiate the driest possible route through the peat hags, a good area for cloudberries in some autumns. When the fence turns sharp L, turn R down to the loch shore and follow the water's edge southwards until the path leading up from the car-park is rejoined.

1 *Grey Mare's Tail*   *Loch Skeen*

During the last Ice Age, when this area was covered in glaciers, the larger, faster glacier in the Moffat Water gouged out a deeper valley than the glacier in the Tail Burn where Loch Skeen now lies. This created a classic 'hanging valley': the Tail Burn must now plunge 200 feet (60 m) to join the Moffat Water.

2 *Charles Lapworth*

Charles Lapworth (1842–1920) is well known to geologists. He lived for a while at Birkhill, the first cottage on the R on the road from the car-park to St Mary's Loch. He made a special study of fossil graptolites here and at Raking Gill beside Birkhill.

3 *Loch Skeen*

The alternative spelling 'Loch Skene' is still sometimes used. At the beginning of the last century white-tailed sea eagles were said to breed here.

In 1962, 2383 acres (964 hectares) of land surrounding the loch were purchased by the National Trust for Scotland, and ten years later a further 128 acres (52 hectares) were added. There is a Ranger service in July and August.

27

2.4

NEW ABBEY and CRIFFEL

STARTING AND
FINISHING
POINT
The Abbey car-
park, New Abbey
(84-964663), 6
miles (9.5 km)
south of Dumfries
on the A710.

LENGTH
6¾ miles (11 km)

ASCENT
1800 ft (550 m)

From the warm-red sandstone ruins of New Abbey, the early part of this walk passes through farmland, mixed and coniferous woodland, and ascends to the heather-clad slopes of Criffel. The summit overlooks the Solway Firth, the last unspoilt major estuary in Europe and the only one with such a fine viewpoint.

ROUTE DESCRIPTION (Map 4)

From the car-park beside Sweetheart Abbey *(1)* go back to the main road and turn R towards the village centre. Turn half L at the Abbey Arms along the road behind the Corn Mill *(2)*. After 40 yards (35 m) turn L so that the mill pond is on your R. The road soon bends to the R and shortly after, on the L, are five granite steps between two yew trees. Go through the kissing-gate to a field, keeping to the L along the hedge to a second such gate. Follow the road ahead for ¾ mile (1.2 km) to a crossroads.

A signpost points the way up to the Waterloo Monument *(3)* but those heading for Criffel should turn L across the sleeper bridge. Pass behind the Mid Glen Cottage, following the rough track beside the tree-lined Glen Burn to a gate and stile. Turn L keeping to the track until it joins a well-defined forest road. Turn R, but leave this road to the L at the second sharp bend, passing along the top of the conifer plantation to a wall. Follow it up the hill for ¾ mile (1.2 km), taking note of a tumbled-down wall that you cross. When the good wall bears L, a fence bears to the R. Bisect the angle between them and follow the ill-defined path through the heather to the summit of Knocken-doch. From here there are good views back to the Abbey and a little to the west of it, among the trees, is Shambellie House *(4)*. Below Knockendoch lies kidney-shaped Loch Kindar *(5)* beyond which is the Nith Estuary.

If visibility is poor there is little point in continuing along the ridge to the summit of Criffel (1867 ft/569 m), but in good conditions the extra mile (1.6 km) will reward the walker with views of Carsethorn *(6)*, the whole of the inner Solway *(7)*, and

Sweetheart Abbey

further afield, the Lake District and Isle of Man.

Return to Knockendoch and descend as far as the previously mentioned fallen wall. Turn L, following the stones down to the forest road (turn half L for the last 10 yards/9 m to avoid the deep ditch). Turn R and follow the roadway for 1½ miles (2.5 km) to the edge of New Abbey. At the edge of the housing estate, turn back half L immediately after passing between two white gate pillars. After 10 yards (9 m) there is a granite stile on the R. Follow the narrow, wooded path behind the houses,

29

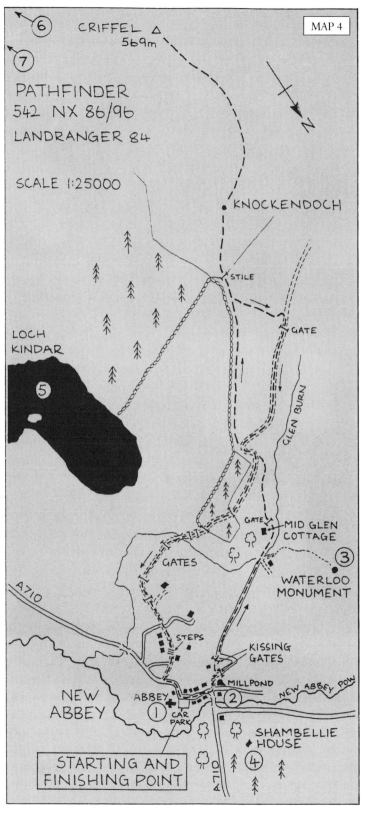

MAP 4

⑥ ← CRIFFEL △
          569m

⑦ ←

PATHFINDER
542 NX 86/96
LANDRANGER 84

SCALE 1:25000

N

● KNOCKENDOCH

STILE

GATE

LOCH
KINDAR

⑤

GLEN BURN

GATE
MID GLEN
COTTAGE

GATES

③
WATERLOO
MONUMENT

A710

STEPS

KISSING
GATES

MILLPOND

NEW ABBEY POW

NEW
ABBEY

ABBEY
① ②
CAR
PARK

SHAMBELLIE
◆ HOUSE

④

A710

STARTING AND
FINISHING POINT

30

descend the twelve stone steps behind an old mill and head between high hedges across the drive to the concrete path which crosses a field to the main road. Cross over the road, turn L, and take the pavement back to the Abbey.

1 *Sweetheart Abbey*
Founded in 1273, the Abbey was 'new' in relation to that of Dundrennan, the mother house founded 130 years earlier 18 miles (29 km) to the south-west. It is known as Sweetheart Abbey because its founder, the widowed Devorgilla Balliol, kept her husband's heart for 16 years in an ivory and silver casket and was buried here with it.

2 *Corn Mill*
There has been a mill on this site since the busy days of the Abbey. The present nineteenth-century mill was in use until 1947 and has recently been restored. The wheel on the west wall is of the high breastshot or pitchback type.

3 *Waterloo Monument*
Construction began on 6 October 1815, less than four months after Napoleon's final defeat. The money was raised by public subscription and the ground was given by William Stewart of Shambellie, whose brother James had commanded the Black Watch 42nd Foot at Waterloo.

4 *Shambellie House*
This Victorian mansion in Scottish baronial style is now a Museum of Costume run by the National Museum of Scotland. It is open from the beginning of July to the end of October.

5 *Loch Kindar*
The larger wooded isle is the site of Kirk Kindar; the smaller is the site of an ancient crannog. Large numbers of mute swans come here in the autumn to moult.

6 *Carsethorn*
This quiet fishing village still boasts a ruinous wooden jetty which recalls its busier days. In 1850 10,000 emigrants left here for Canada and 11,000 for Australia and New Zealand.

7 *Solway Firth*
The mudflats and adjacent saltmarshes of the inner Solway are of international importance as the feeding grounds for several species of geese, ducks and waders. The entire population of barnacle geese from Spitzbergen, in the Norwegian islands of Svalbard, winters here, mainly at Caerlaverock and Rockcliffe Marshes. More than 20,000 oystercatchers spend mid-winter on these shores.

3·5

THE MERRICK

STARTING AND
FINISHING
POINT
Bruce's Stone car-
park, Glentrool
(77-415804). At
Bargrennan turn
north off the A714
to Glentrool village.
Turn east for 3¾
miles (6 km) to the
end of the metalled
road.

LENGTH
10 miles (16 km)

ASCENT
2300 ft (700 m).

After climbing to the highest point in southern Scotland, the return route skirts the shores of three rugged hill lochs then descends the slopes of Glentrool to finish with a delightful oak-lined section with a waterfall. The walk provides a good introduction to the Galloway hills but here and elsewhere in the Southern Uplands the difficulties should not be underestimated.

ROUTE DESCRIPTION (Maps 5, 6)

Follow the path northwards from Bruce's Stone *(1)* along the west side of the Buchan Burn. The early part of the way is signposted so there should be no difficulty. At the second stile the route passes through a conifer plantation for ½ mile (800 m) until the ruin of Culsharg is reached. Go to the left of the building, heading uphill to a forest road. Turn R across the concrete bridge but 25 yards (20 m) later turn L up a gravelly slope into the trees once more.

After the stile above the trees continue upwards to a wall, turning R to follow it to the top of Benyellary. On good days the Mull of Galloway, Ailsa Craig and Arran can be seen.

From Benyellary continue beside the wall for ⅝ mile (1 km) then turn half R along the faint path which leads to the Merrick summit (2770 ft/843 m).

East of the Merrick there is a wonderful assortment of waters. Loch Doon to the north and Clatteringshaws to the south-east were both artificially dammed in the 1930s as part of the Galloway hydro-electric scheme. Closer to hand, Loch Enoch *(2)* and her sister lochs give this area its special beauty.

There is no path for the descent to the fence at the south-west corner of Loch Enoch, but the vegetation is short and easily managed if care is taken. At the stile by the shore a 400-yard (375 m) diversion up the fence will give, after a little searching, a sighting of the Grey Man of the Merrick.

Returning to the loch, turn R and walk along the shore until it heads northwards abruptly. Turn R here and follow the

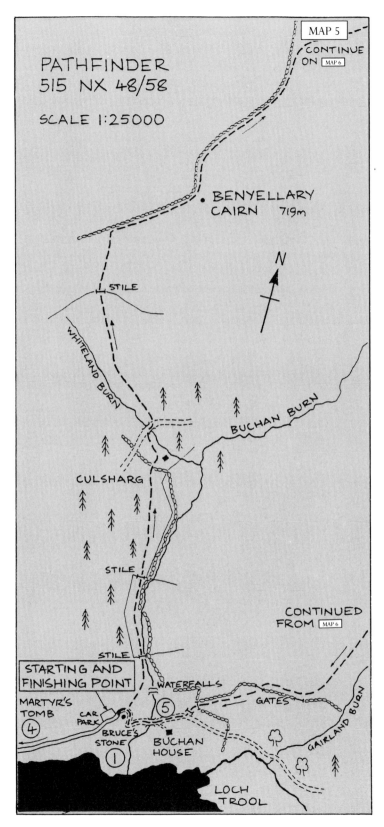

PATHFINDER
515 NX 48/58

SCALE 1:25000

MAP 5

CONTINUE
ON MAP 6

BENYELLARY
CAIRN 719m

N

STILE

WHITELAND BURN

BUCHAN BURN

CULSHARG

STILE

CONTINUED
FROM MAP 6

STILE

STARTING AND
FINISHING POINT

WATERFALLS

GATES

GAIRLAND BURN

MARTYR'S
TOMB

CAR
PARK

BRUCE'S
STONE

BUCHAN
HOUSE

LOCH
TROOL

4

5

1

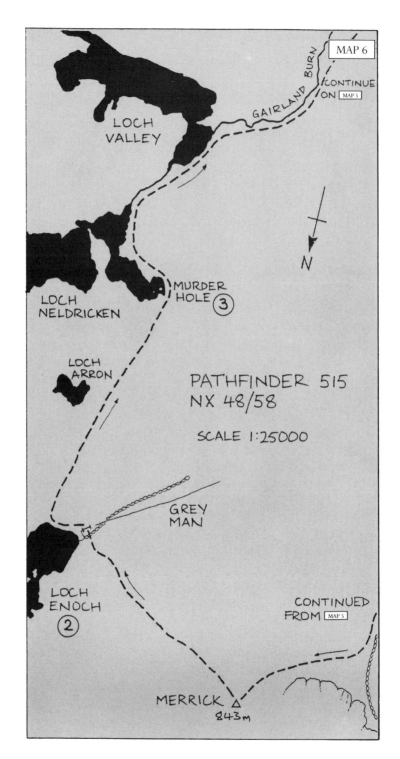

MAP 6

narrow pass towards Loch Neldricken. The path now becomes obvious again. Skirt to the west of the Murder Hole *(3)* and follow the path towards Loch Valley, afterwards keeping to the west bank of the Gairland Burn. The route is wet in places, but

the path improves as it begins to contour around the side of *Buchan Burn*
Buchan Hill to a wall. Just off the path, the rocky knoll beyond
the gate is a good view-point for Loch Trool. In the woods at
the far end is the Martyrs' Tomb at Caldons *(4)*.

The path back remains on the north side of the wall for 250 yards (225 m) then enters the field by a small gate. Turn half R and go downhill to the field corner, where there is another small gate. At the stile beside the next gate turn R along the track which leads through the oak woods back to Bruce's Stone. It is worth pausing at the Buchan Bridge *(5)* and for those with the energy a 200-yard (180-m) excursion up the path on the east bank leads to one of Galloway's most spectacular waterfalls.

1 *Bruce's Stone*

The large granite boulder is inscribed: 'In loyal remembrance of Robert the Bruce, King of Scots, whose victory in this glen over an English force in March, 1307, opened the campaign of independence which he brought to a decisive close at Bannockburn on 24th June, 1314.'

The stone was erected in 1929, 600 years after Bruce's death. The battle took place on the other side of the loch, where a small band of Scots hurled boulders down the hillside and routed Sir Aymer de Valence's 2,000 men.

2 *Loch Enoch*

The silver sand from the loch's beaches was once prized as a coating for greased wooden hone sticks, used for sharpening scythes.

A feature of this loch is an island with its own lochan.

3 *The Murder Hole*

This marshy dark-water bay of Loch Neldricken features in S. R. Crockett's novel *The Raiders* as a site for concealing stolen goods and the bodies of the thieves' victims. The Galloway-born author's other works include *Men of the Moss Hags* and *Mad Sir Uchtred.*

4 *The Martyrs' Tomb*

South-west Scotland was the scene of many bloody acts during the 'Killing Times'. Seventeenth-century Scottish Presbyterians objected to having the English Episcopalian form of worship thrust upon them, so their leaders signed the rebellious National Covenant in 1638. Many took to the hills to hold their services. The Martyrs' Tomb commemorates six such Covenanters surprised at prayer and shot by dragoons.

5 *Buchan Bridge*

This small sandstone bridge was designed by Randolph, 9th Earl of Galloway. Part of the inscription alludes, in the words of Sir Walter Scott, to the surrounding 'Land of the Brown Heath and Shaggy Wood, Land of the Mountain and the Flood.'

3·6

THE MINCHMOOR ROAD

Much of the Border country is rich in history and this area is no exception. The route is mainly a ridge walk along an old drove road (and the Southern Upland Way) from Traquair to the Three Brethren. The return via Broadmeadows makes use of the Minchmoor Road. The path surface is generally excellent.

ROUTE DESCRIPTION (Maps 7–9)

From Traquair village hall turn L away from the main road uphill for 150 yards (140 m) until the road bends to the R. Continue straight ahead, following the rough trackway signposted 'Minchmoor'. Carry on up between the widely spaced walls of the old drove road which led to Galashiels and Selkirk. The route should now be clear for 7 miles (11 km) all the way to the Three Brethren, since Southern Upland Way *(1)* signs clarify any doubtful sections.

At 1500 ft (460 m) the track starts to contour round the heathery north side of Minch Moor, 1859 ft (567 m), passing just to the left of the ancient Cheese Well *(2)*. Continue along the ridge for 1½ miles (2.5 km) to Hare Law where the drove road and Minchmoor Road divide. Fork L, continuing to follow the Southern Upland Way signs. After ½ mile (800 m) the track passes through an ancient ditch and embankment known as Wallace's Trench *(3)*.

Beyond Brown Knowe the path becomes narrow and descends to a ladder stile at the west end of a windblown shelter belt of larch and pine. Keeping the trees on your R, carry on eastwards along the grassy track which skirts to the north of Broomy Law, enjoying all the while the open views of the rolling Border hills.

At the new plantation which appears on the L, follow the rough track until it joins a well-used forest road which leads up to the Three Brethren: three tall, closely placed cairns, each on ground of different ownership. As you look eastwards, the best views of the three Eildon Hills are now obtained.

A Southern Upland Way fingerpost indicates the route

STARTING AND FINISHING POINT
Traquair village-hall car-park (73-332346). Turn L off the B709 from Innerleithen at the Traquair war memorial. The village hall is 100 yards (90 m) along on the L.

LENGTH
16 miles (26 km)

ASCENT
2300 ft (700 m)

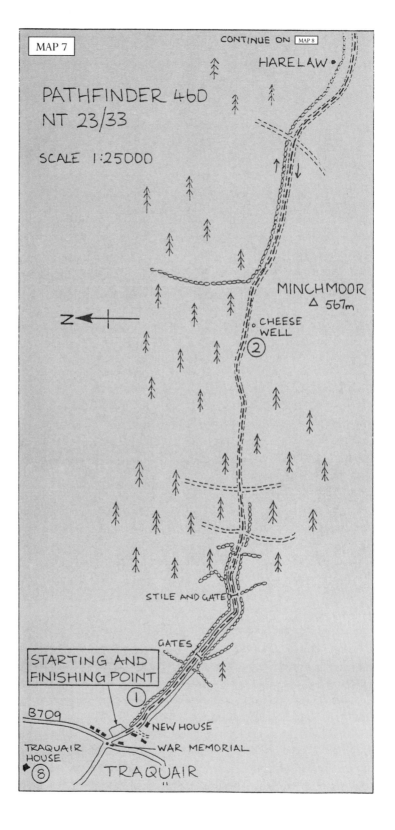

downhill to the R, but as the Way bears L into the trees, turn R *The Three Brethren*
through the gate. Join the track beside the gate, turn R along it
for 10 yards (9 m), then turn R again to double back almost
parallel to the fence, but veer slightly L from it. The path ahead
is very overgrown with heather but after 500 yards (450 m)
there is a gate beyond which the track is clearly visible, and it
remains so. From the col ahead there is a steep descent from the
high moors down to the Yarrow valley, to a small wood where a
L turn leads directly towards the ruins of Newark Castle *(4)*.

From the gate beside the A708 it is only ¼ mile (400 m)
eastwards to Foulshiels, the ruined birthplace of the explorer
Mungo Park *(5)*, but those walkers keeping to the route should
turn R into Broadmeadows *(6)*, crossing two bridges over the
Yarrow Water twice within ¼ mile (400 m).

From the second bridge it is 600 yards (550 m) until the
Minchmoor is signposted to the R. The narrow road soon
becomes a rough track which leads up behind some red-roofed
garages. Turn L at the first junction, beside some magnificent
old beech trees. Once above the trees turn L along the north
side of the wood and enjoy the gentle uphill gradient of the old
Minchmoor Road *(7)*, with its splendid wide grassy surface,
open outlook and historic associations with the past.

At Hare Law rejoin the Southern Upland Way and follow it
back to Traquair. By now walkers will be travelling at a more
leisurely pace than that of the Marquis of Montrose when he
fled along the Minchmoor Road on his way to Traquair House
(8). The house may be glimpsed among the trees on the descent
to the finishing point.

1. Southern Upland Way
This 212-mile (340-km) coast-to-coast long-distance footpath traverses some of Dumfries and Galloway's finest
scenery. Starting in the west at Portpatrick, it passes through

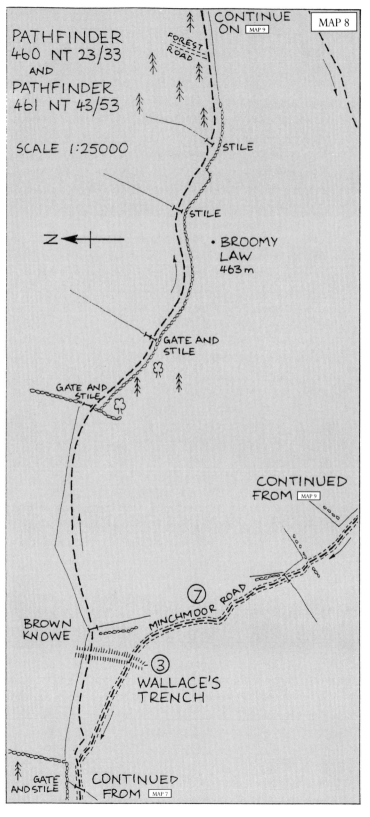

PATHFINDER
460 NT 23/33
AND
PATHFINDER
461 NT 43/53

SCALE 1:25000

CONTINUE
ON MAP 9

FOREST ROAD

MAP 8

STILE

STILE

• BROOMY LAW 463 m

GATE AND STILE

GATE AND STILE

CONTINUED FROM MAP 9

⑦

MINCHMOOR ROAD

BROWN KNOWE

③
WALLACE'S TRENCH

GATE AND STILE

CONTINUED FROM MAP 7

40

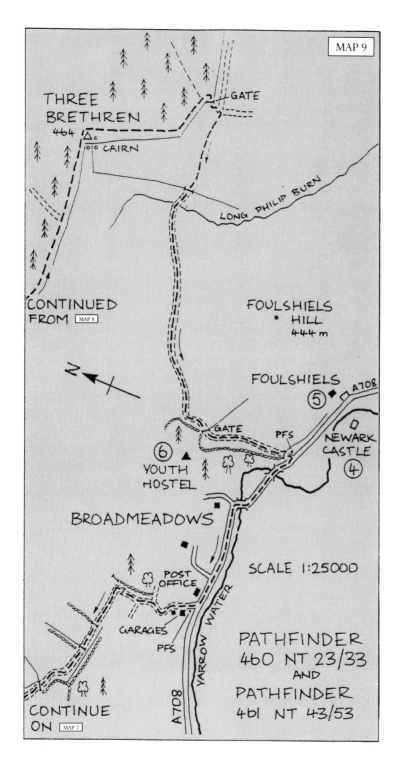

MAP 9

THREE
BRETHREN
464
CAIRN
GATE

LONG PHILIP BURN

CONTINUED
FROM MAP 8

FOULSHIELS
• HILL
444 m

N

FOULSHIELS
⑤
A708

GATE
PFS
NEWARK
CASTLE
④

⑥
YOUTH
HOSTEL

BROADMEADOWS

POST
OFFICE

SCALE 1:25000

GARAGES
PFS

YARROW WATER

A708

PATHFINDER
460 NT 23/33
AND
PATHFINDER
461 NT 43/53

CONTINUE
ON MAP 7

Castle Kennedy, Glentrool, St John's Town of Dalry, Sanquhar, Wanlockhead and Beattock before heading into the borders to finish at Cockburnspath, overlooking the North Sea.

2 *Cheese Well*

The spring is marked by two stones, one dated 1965, the other much older. By tradition travellers made an offering of cheese to placate the fairies or spirits of the well, to ensure protection on the Minchmoor Road.

3 *Wallace's Trench*

This linear earthwork lies across both the Minchmoor Road and the old drove road. It may have had an administrative rather than defensive purpose and probably had no connection with the popular hero William Wallace.

4 *Newark Castle*

The courtyard of this fifteenth-century square tower was the scene of a dreadful slaughter of Royalist prisoners after the Battle of Philiphaugh in 1645. Much later, it was visited by Sir Walter Scott and William Wordsworth together, and featured in Scott's *Lay of the Last Minstrel*.

5 *Mungo Park*

Born in 1771, Park studied medicine in Edinburgh and between his two African expeditions practised in Peebles 13 miles (21 km) north-west of Foulshiels. There were no white survivors of his second great journey (in 1806) but Park is believed to have drowned in the Niger while being attacked by natives.

6 *Broadmeadows*

The Scottish Youth Hostel Association is responsible for over 80 hostels. The first to be opened, in 1931, was at Broadmeadows, the opening party crossing the Minchmoor to complete the ceremony.

7 *The Minchmoor Road*

This trackway has been in use since at least the thirteenth century as it was part of the road between Kelso Abbey and its lands at Lesmahagow. In 1296 Edward I and his army used the road during his campaign against the Scots.

Four centuries later, the Marquis of Montrose galloped along this road to bang on the door of Traquair House, after his defeat at Philiphaugh by General Leslie's Covenanting army. He was refused admission but eventually escaped to Norway.

8 *Traquair House*

Visited by twenty-seven kings, Traquair House claims to be the oldest inhabited house in Scotland. The main block dates from 1642, about the time that the 1st Earl of Traquair diverted the course of the River Tweed to prevent the foundations from being undermined.

SELECTED WALKS IN THE SOUTHERN AND CENTRAL HIGHLANDS AND CAIRNGORMS

Rennie McOwan

Glen Coe

INTRODUCTION

Asked to select six walks of varying lengths in an area south of the Great Glen and more or less to the north of a line between Edinburgh and Glasgow, I was faced with an embarrassment of riches. How could I leave out the linking summits of the Mamores, the main peaks of the Cairngorms, the Monadh Liath, Creag Meaghaidh, Ben Alder and the hills around Loch Ossian and Loch Treig? The same reluctance was evoked by the thought of the round tops of the Drumochter Pass, cone-shaped Schiehallion, the Glen Coe hills, the attractive peaks at Arrochar, the Loch Tay-side and Glen Lyon hills, and many other fine walks.

In an attempt to overcome this near-impossible task I have concentrated on routes which are fulfilling in themselves and which can also provide walkers with an introduction to an area. These walks are both a foretaste and a full meal. Each can be enjoyed for its own sake once its character and status has been identified and appreciated and yet each opens a door to wider horizons.

Scotland has several hills of a near-mystical character, but perhaps none more so than Bennachie, much beloved of north-east folk and with a history which far outweighs its size. It is a tasty morsel on a rich plate. The same is true of Dunchuach, at Inveraray, famous in clan legend. Both of these small hills are ideal for family scrambles or afternoon or evening walks. Ben Nevis has to be included because it is Britain's biggest mountain, but the route includes views of its often hidden and magnificent cliffs.

Two classic Cairngorms passes are chosen: the Lairig Ghru through the main plateau and the Tolmount, which connects Glen Clova and Braemar. Both are rich in tales and legends and offer views to other hills. Both are major walks. The two Glen Coe passes, the Lairig Eilde and the Lairig Gartain, are pleasant walks in themselves, besides serving as an introduction to Glen Coe.

All such choices are subjective. But if they make you come back, then that is what they were meant to do. Happy walking!

1·7

Dun na Cuaiche (Dunchuach) Hill, Inveraray

This walk and the drive to Inveraray (pronounced *Inver-air-ah*), the old capital of Clan Campbell and home of the Duke of Argyll, give something of the flavour of the fine hills and the turbulent history of what used to be known as 'shire Argile'.

The small hill of Dunchuach (pronounced *Dun-whoo-ich*) overlooking Inveraray Castle, has an almost mystical appeal. It offers fine views down Loch Fyne and to the surrounding hills and glens, as well as to the inlet loch of Loch Shira at its foot. The ascent is made through attractive woodland and there is a circular return. The paths have been discreetly waymarked by the Argyll estates, and the 'blue' route to the summit and back, lasting about 2½–3 hours, is by far the best walk.

STARTING AND FINISHING POINT
Inveraray Castle car-park (56-095094). Turn off the A83 at Inveraray town.

LENGTH
2½ miles (4 km)

ASCENT
800 ft (240 m)

Route Description (Map 10)

From the car-park at Inveraray Castle *(1)* follow the estate road across a bridge and the River Aray in a northerly direction. Passing attractive trees, some of them commemorating the visit by Queen Victoria to the castle in 1875, go straight across a field in the direction of large coniferous trees to a green gate. Please shut the gate. You are now in an old arboretum *(2)*. The route continues past the remains of a lime kiln, the product of which was used in past times as fertilizer. It is best to view these buildings from nearby and not to climb over them. A short walk branches off from here, but you continue upwards on the blue route.

Turn sharp R and follow the old road for 25 yards (20 metres) then turn sharp L and proceed up hill. These woods are rich in flowers and insects and there is a wide variety of birds. The woods are particularly attractive in spring when the bluebells (wild hyacinths) are out. Through a gap in the trees, a

45

tall circular building, a dovecote built in 1748, can be seen in the middle distance *(3)*.

Turn L on the blue route and there is a short section of single-track footpath leading to a level section of the track from which there are good views *(4)*. The path continues in an easterly direction towards Loch Fyne and you soon reach a view-point for the castle, the town and the surrounding area. There is some scree here—rocks broken up by the action of frost and water—and as it can slide easily you should stick carefully to the path.

The route then turns sharply L and goes uphill. The terrain changes from woodland to near-moorland and then to hill, with birches and heather, rushes and grasses. Continue uphill until you pick up the line of an old road to the top. This is known as *Glac a' Bharaille* ('the hollow of the barrel'). Follow this old road to the summit and its folly in the form of a tower *(5)*. Rest and enjoy the view and try to discern the many layers of history which have shaped this landscape *(6)*.

Take the longer, blue route back down by returning to point 15 and then following the signs. (Do not turn R and return the way you came up.) On reaching the first road proceed downhill to the right for about 100 yards (90 m) and then turn sharp L and follow the footpath through the woods. You will pass a seat, known locally as the 'sweetie seat' (a place for courting and sucking sweets, a courting gift in past times), with fine views. Continue along the section known as the 'Grand Approach' to the castle and then leave the road and descend steeply to the River Aray. Follow the track up the river for about 150 yards (140 m) to return to your starting-point.

1 Inveraray Castle

The Campbells of Argyll were mainly winners in Scottish history and supported the House of Hanover against the exiled House of Stuart. It is a sign of their confidence that the present Inveraray Castle was started by Archibald, the 3rd Duke of Argyll, in the middle of the unsuccessful 1745 Jacobite Rising. It was completed by the 5th Duke 40 years later and replaced a fifteenth-century castle. Four white stones in the field near the car-park mark the older fortification. The new castle was designed by Roger Morris and the construction was supervised by William Adam, father of the architects John, Robert and James. It has fine furnishings and memorabilia of Clan Campbell.

Opposite *View from the Folly Tower to Inveraray Castle*

2 *The Arboretum*

The Argyll family were pioneers in landscaping and forestry as early as the seventeenth century. In this collection of trees are Japanese larch grafted into a European root stock, Japanese cedar, Wellingtonia (named after the Duke of Wellington, who died just before it was 'discovered' in 1841), East Himalayan fir, Algerian fir, western hemlock, grand fir, European silver fir and Japanese yezo or hondo spruce. The Argyll estates produce a booklet identifying the trees.

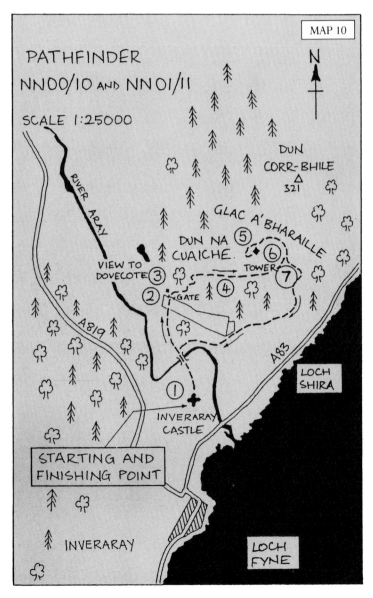

3 *Dovecote*

This was built in 1748 as part of the 3rd Duke's plan for his estate. Dovecotes were a common feature of Scottish estates and in earlier centuries Lowland landowners were urged by law to build them; an invader could burn houses and crops and kill or steal livestock, but pigeons were harder to deal with. In the Highlands a lack of feeding led to dovecotes being restricted to owners who could feed the birds, so that neighbours were not troubled. The author Neil Munro made the dovecote a central location in his historical novel *The New Road*, described by John Buchan as the best historical novel since those of Sir Walter Scott. However, the dovecote was built almost thirty years after the 1719 Jacobite Rising.

4 *Views*

As you climb higher you can see how important Dunchuach was to the Campbells as a view-point. Three main glens radiate north from Inveraray—Glen Aray, Glen Fyne and Glen Shira—and Clan Campbell always believed they could block the head of these passes against enemies. And so they could against armies with baggage and cannon. But they were caught out in 1645 in the Scottish Wars of the Covenant when the Royalist army of the Marquis of Montrose and his second-in-command, the war leader of Clan Donald, Alasdair MacColla, sent their fast-moving Gaelic troops through the winter hills. Inveraray was captured and sacked.

5 *The Folly Tower*

This building looks ancient and occurs in Neil Munro's novel, *John Splendid,* when he depicts the Campbell garrison being besieged by Montrose's clansmen. This, alas, was an anachronism—a failing of which Neil Munro was often guilty. The folly is sited so that when seen from the castle and town it is silhouetted against the sky. It was built by Roger Morris and William Adam in 1748 for the then large sum of £46 and was designed to look like a ruin from below.

6 *The Summit*

The name *Dun Na Cuaiche* (Dunchuach) means 'the fort of the cup (or bowl)', probably because of the bowl shape at the top. An Iron Age rampart can also be traced. The neighbouring hill is Duntorvil, a corruption of the Gaelic *Corr-bhile,* meaning 'the (highest) eminence on the ridge'. The wild hill land roundabout is worth scrutiny. Ben Buidhe, ('the yellow mountain') can be seen to the north-east and from the north side of the summit you see one of the great mountains of Scotland, Ben Cruachan (pronounced *Croo-ichin*). In Gaelic this is Cruachan Beann ('the heaped-up hill of the many tops'), the two main summits of which are seen from many parts of the Southern and Central Highlands. Ben Cruachan gave Clan Campbell its war slogan (*'Cruachan!'*) and should be earmarked by all hillwalkers for a future visit. The traverse of all its peaks makes a fine expedition, but it is a mountain which deserves care and respect. A hydro-electric dam, built between 1961 and 1966, can just be picked out in its central corrie. The hills around Arrochar and Loch Long, Ben Ime and its neighbours, Ben Narnain and the Cobbler, should also be borne in mind for the future.

7 *Rhododendrons*

The shrub was introduced to Britain from Turkey in 1753, and the name means 'the tree of Rhodes from the land on Pontus'. Other varieties come from the Himalayas and the Far East. Its colourful flowers in June bring joy to many, but it is also a problem because it forms dense thickets which block other plants and, unless kept in check, can block paths and forest rides. Argyll's high rainfall and acid soil suit its growth but, unfortunately, it also sours the soil and creates conditions favourable to its own spread.

Inveraray Folly

1·8

BENNACHIE

Bennachie (pronounced *Bain-a-hee*) is one of Scotland's best known mystical hills, a prominent landmark from many parts of Aberdeenshire and dominating the farmlands of the Garioch (pronounced *Gay-ree*) and Buchan. Some historians think that the famous battle of Mons Graupius in AD 84 or 85 took place here. It was then that the invading Romans defeated the Caledonian tribes and their leader Calgacus uttered the famous words: 'They make a desert and they call it peace.'

The Rowan Tree route to the Mither Tap is traditionally the most popular, but it is not the best. That honour belongs to this route, starting at Esson's Croft car-park.

STARTING AND FINISHING POINT
Esson's Croft car-park (38-700217)

LENGTH
3½ miles (5 km)

ASCENT
1200 ft (370 m)

ACCESS

At the village of Kemnay, on the River Don, turn off the B993 on to the Fetternear-Blairdaff road, called Riverside Road. Continue on this road for 2 miles (3 km), then turn R on to the Blairdaff-Chapel of Garioch road. After 1 mile (1.6 km), turn R on to the Chapel of Garioch road. From there drive a further 2 miles (3 km) and find the entrance to the Esson's Croft car-park, marked 'Forest Walks' on the L.

ROUTE DESCRIPTION (Map 11)

From Esson's Croft car-park take the path by the map board, with the toilets on the R. After ¼ mile (400 m), with the Clachie Burn on the L, the path veers R and then L to a fork. Take the L fork and after 50 yards (45 m), turn R at the sign to the Gouk Stone *(1)*. Return to the fork in the track.

Continue for 200 yards (180 m) to where there is a seat and the track branches into three. Take the track to the R and follow it for 200 yards (180 m) out of the trees to Esson's Croft *(2)*. Pass the ruins and after 100 yards (90 m) turn L at the 'T' junction. Continue ahead to the gate and after another 50 yards (45 m) turn R on to the footpath. Follow the path uphill as it meanders out of the trees and on to the summit of 'Mither Tap'

51

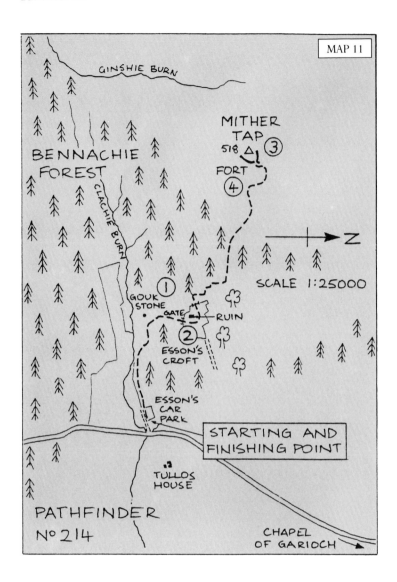

MAP 11

GINSHIE BURN

MITHER
TAP
518 △ ③

BENNACHIE
FOREST

FORT
④

CLACHIE BURN

N

SCALE 1:25000

GOUK ①
STONE
GATE — RUIN
②
ESSON'S
CROFT

ESSON'S
CAR
PARK

STARTING AND
FINISHING POINT

TULLOS
HOUSE

PATHFINDER
Nº 214

CHAPEL
OF GARIOCH

(3), a distance of ¾ mile (1.2 km). Near the top the track passes
through the outer walls of an Iron Age fort *(4)*. Carefully
scramble on to the summit tor, where there is an indicator. This
rocky tor is very precipitous on its north and west sides. Return
by the same route *(5)*.

1 The Gouk Stone

Ruined walls in a clearing tell an old and sad story and so
does this small standing stone, although it has no markings or
carvings. It was a marker stone showing the boundary of
common land divided by court action in 1859. At the start of
the nineteenth century, some tenacious local people, who

became known as The Colonists, created crofts for themselves on unpromising land of scrub and heather. Also working as hired help on the bigger farms of the lower ground, they won a living by hard toil and courage. But eight neighbouring estates began a court action in 1844 to divide up the common land between them, and the squatters then became tenants whether they liked it or not. Rent rises over the years eventually forced all the families but one to leave. *Gouk* or *Gowk* is a Scots word for a cuckoo (although it can also mean a fool) and the stone may have been a favourite perching place for this bird in April.

2 *Esson's Croft*

When the squatters or colonists were squeezed off the land they had won in the face of such adversity, George Esson alone refused to admit defeat. He struggled on and died there in 1938 and the ruins of the croft still bear his name. It is fitting that the car-park at the start of this walk should carry his name, for he deserves to be remembered. Keep a look out for inscribed stones with initials and nineteenth-century

Easter Aquhorthies Stone Circle with Bennachie looming in the distance

dates. They were erected by the estates which took over the colonists' crofts, to make clear their ownership. One stone is dated '1858', a year in advance of the court's decision. The estate owners must have been very confident of gaining the disputed land.

3 *Mither Tap*

Bennachie forms a ridge 3 miles (5 km) long, with a series of tops of which the highest is the Oxen (pronounced *Ow-sin*) Craig (1733 ft/528 m). However, the best known and the most attractive summit to ascend is the slightly lower and easternmost point, called the Mither Tap. It is a great cap of granite and although the name is obscure, as is the derivation of Bennachie, it may mean 'the mother-top'. It certainly has something of a matriarchal air about it.

4 *The Fort*

Some authorities say the ancient fort on top of the Mither Tap is a vitrified fort (that is, the walls have been fused by heat and fire) but this is incorrect. Its origins are shadowy, but it is thought to be from between 500 BC and AD 500, the Iron Age. Many tons of stones were brought up the hill to build this fort and within the existing walls were at least ten buildings and a well, now dry.

5 *Return Journey*

This ascent is recommended as an introduction to Bennachie. The views from the Mither Tap and the summit are extensive, to the hills of Caithness, the Cairngorms, around Glen Clova and over the farmlands. It might seem strange to recommend a route which does not go to the summit, but this is a special hill of great character and its qualities cannot be fully appreciated, even on several visits.

2·9

GLEN COE

This circular walk goes through two attractive passes running from Glen Coe to Glen Etive and forms a pleasant introduction to the Glen Coe area.

ROUTE DESCRIPTION (Map 12)

The Lairig Eilde (pronounced *Eel-che*) *(1)* to Glen Etive is a right-of-way and is signposted on the south side of the A82 and to the east of the area and waterfall known as The Study. There is room for only a few cars on the north side of the road close to a prominent cairn and to the start of the walk, but further west more parking space can be found. Take great care when walking on the road, one of the busiest in the Highlands.

A tiny path goes over moundy ground on the L (east) side of the burn, the Allt Lairig Eilde, and although it partly continues on this side it is better to cross the burn to the R (west) side where another path is more clearly defined.

On your R (west) are the steep slopes of Beinn Fhada (the second word is pronounced *atta*) the first of the prominent rocky, roadside peaks in Glen Coe known collectively as the Three Sisters. On your L (east) are the slopes of Buachaille Etive Beag *(2)*, a long ridge of a hill which runs from Stob nan Cabar over Stob Coire Raineach to Stob Dubh in the south.

Proceed gradually uphill on a path which has been occasionally cairned, a reprehensible practice *(3)*, with the craggy faces of Stob Coire Sgreamhach, a linked peak to Bidean (pronounced *Bitchen*) nam Bian, the highest mountain in Argyll, half R and starting to dominate the pass. Look out for deer on both sides of the pass at this stage: the area was once a royal hunting forest. There is no problem with deer stalkers: this is National Trust for Scotland ground and, other than a cull, no shooting takes place. The sight and sound of traffic vanishes as you ascend.

At the end of the pass is a cairn and the route then turns due south. Just over the crest of the pass and as you descend to Glen

STARTING AND FINISHING POINT
Car-parking space in Glen Coe near The Study waterfall on the A82 to Fort William (41-189568).

LENGTH
9 miles (14 km)

ASCENT
500 ft (150 m) at the crest of each of the two passes, the Lairig Eilde and the Lairig Gartain.

Etive you will see a prominent, flat-topped stone *(4)* on which a land-boundary deal was signed in clan times. Descend sharply downhill towards the estate lodge of Dalness *(5)*, with good views opening up of lovely Glen Etive. At this point you have a choice of route.

Dalness is private land and was once the reputed site of the legendary Deirdre's bower. It can be viewed only from the hillside and the very nimble need not descend completely to the single-track road which runs past Dalness down Glen Etive and ends at the disused pier at the head of Loch Etive. It is possible to contour the hillside westwards into the return pass, the Lairig Gartain, but this is recommended only for those who are comfortable crossing steep ground. Otherwise, descend to the road where the signposted start of the Lairig Gartain begins and prepare to ascend once again. The Lairig Gartain *(6)* runs north-eastwards from this point on the road.

The pull uphill is steep, but there is a reasonable path which starts to vanish in the upper reaches. It is worth stopping for good views back down Glen Etive to distant Loch Etive and also to see the extent to which modern forestry now cloaks a once-fertile glen *(7)*.

Over the crest of the pass the ground is more featureless, but there is an intermittent path which follows the line of the River Coupall, where there are some fine pools. On your R (east) is the long ridge of that fine mountain the Buachaille Etive Mor *(8)*. Again, keep an eye out for deer. The track reaches the A82 to the west of Lagangarbh mountaineering cottage: be sure to

Glen Coe

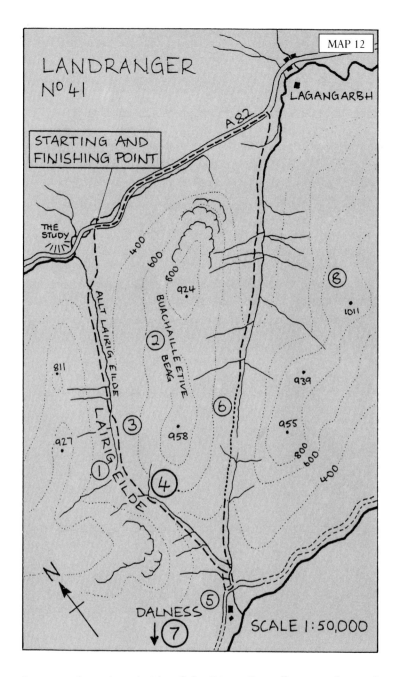

MAP 12

LANDRANGER
Nº 41

STARTING AND
FINISHING POINT

LAGANGARBH

THE STUDY

A82

400
600
600

924

BUACHAILLE ETIVE BEAG

811

ALLT LAIRIG EILDE

LAIRIG EILDE

927

③

①

④

958

⑦

⑥

⑥

939

955

800
600
400

⑧

1011

N

DALNESS ⑤

↓⑦

SCALE 1:50,000

keep on the L (west) side of the River Coupall as you descend.
You then walk westwards for about 2 miles (3 km) along the
A82 back to your vehicle. Do be careful of cars on this road.

1 *Pass of the Hinds—the Lairig Eilde*

The word 'lairig' simply means a pass and the Gaelic word
eilde means hinds, female deer. It is thus 'the pass of the
hinds'. This was a well-used hill crossing from Glen Coe in
the past and was possibly used as an escape route by the

MacDonalds (MacIains) in the notorious 1692 massacre, although it is about a mile (1.6 km) from the start of the site of the old MacDonald townships and about 4 miles (6.5 km) from where most of the others were sited.

2 *Buachaille Etive Beag*

The little herdsman of Etive, as the name may be translated, shelters the pass on the east and its long ridge comprises three subsidiary peaks. The one nearest the road, Stob nan Cabar, means 'the peak of the *cabar*', the tree-trunk tossed in Highland games, the next (running south-east) is Stob Coire Raineach ('the peak of the ferns or bracken'), and Stob Dubh ('black peak'). Gaelic hill names often give an idea of the terrain.

3 *Cairning*

The National Trust for Scotland's mountaineering benefactor, the late Percy Unna, drew up enlightened rules for the management of hill property. (He also led financial appeals and gave generously himself to enable the Trust to acquire several mountain properties.) These rules included: no man-made structures on the hills, no facilities for food or drink, no new paths to be constructed, the mountains not to be made easier or safer to climb, and no access for wheeled vehicles. His achievements are attracting increasing attention nowadays as conservation issues reach wider audiences. He detested the cairning of paths and when he found a cairn he kicked it down. Stob Coire Sgreamhach means 'the peak of the rocky corrie'. As a corrie is a kettle—not like the modern handle-and-spout kind, but bowl-shaped—the name indicates a big hollow or saucer-shape in the hills.

4 *Clachan Reamhair*

A cluster of large boulders encountered as you descend from the crest of the pass is known as the Clachan Reamhair ('the traveller's village'). They gave shelter to wanderers. Just before you reach these stones there is a flat stone known as Clach an t-Suidhe ('the stone of the seat'). Campbell of Inverawe signed title deeds of Dalness on this stone in stiff discussions with the MacDonalds of Dalness, whose clanspeople were a sept linked to the MacDonalds (MacIains) of Glen Coe, and who were suspicious of Clan Campbell's expansionist policies.

5 *Dalness*

Now a shooting estate, this was once a Clan Donald holding. Neil Munro brought the house into his historical novel *John Splendid*, telling how a band of Campbell fugitives returning *Opposite Dalness* from the battle of Inverlochy in 1645 were almost trapped by the MacDonalds. A gun reputed to have been used in the killing of Colin Campbell of Glen Ure in the period following the 1745 Jacobite Rising was kept at Dalness for a time. Robert Louis Stevenson used this killing, known as the Appin murder, in *Kidnapped*, when Colin Campbell was shot by an unknown sniper while on his way to evict the Stewart tenants who had supported the Jacobites. Stevenson called Colin Campbell the Red Fox and the gun was known as the Black Gun of Misfortune because an innocent man, James Stewart of the Glens, was hanged for the murder. The killer of the Red Fox remains an enduring Scottish mystery.

6 *The Lairig Gartain*

This was another popular hill crossing in past centuries. Seen from the A82, the crest of the pass shows a lovely scallop shape between the two Buachailles. Gartain is a man's name and this whole corner is still known as the Royal Forest of Dalness and marked on the maps as such. Great deer hunts sometimes involved hundreds of men and the deer were driven into enclosures or 'box canyons', called *elrigs*, and then killed by spear, sword and axe. The Dalness area was popular with Scottish kings in past times and much political discussion took place at such hunt gatherings.

7 *Glen Etive*

The glen was once very fertile and supported many townships, but is now given over to hill farming and forestry. The name *etive* derives from a word for an old Celtic storm goddess. Loch Etive is almost 18 miles (29 km) long and is tidal. It is flanked by fine mountains, worth noting for future exploration, including Ben Starav ('the strong mountain') and Ben Trilleachan ('mountain of sandpipers') beloved of slab rock-climbers, but which can also be ascended by walkers from Loch Etive-side. Another fine walk runs down the north shore of Loch Etive to Dail and Cadderlie, a reputed Deirdre bower site (see below), on an island, and where there was once an ancient orchard.

An old Scottish and Irish Gaelic legend tells of Deirdre of the Sorrows and how she and her lover Naoise (pronounced *Noy-sha*) lived a life of Golden Age joy in different parts of the Highlands and had a special haven or bower in Glen Etive. Deirdre was lured by the jealous King Conchobar of Ulster back to Ireland, where she and Naoise were killed. Tribal war broke out as a result, thus fulfilling an ancient prophecy that Naoise's family, the House of Uisnach (pronounced *Wish-na*),

Opposite Waterfall below The Study

60

would be the cause of the fall of the House of Ulster. Deirdre is regarded as the Celtic Helen and the Gaelic people in centuries past believed the old tale to be true.

8 *Buachaille Etive Mor*

'The great herdsman of Etive' is one of the best-known mountains of Scotland, with its main, sharp-pointed peak, Stob Dearg (pronounced *Stob Jerrack*) ('the red peak') dominating the road from the south. Like its neighbour, Buachaille Etive Beag, it sends a long ridge running to the south-east and which ends in Stob na Broige ('the peak of the shoe'), from which the word 'brogue' comes. Its steep slopes hide the top peaks when the walker is in the Lairig Gartain, but its closeness, and that of its neighbour, Buachaille Etive Beag, and the views all round from the passes, provide a good introduction to the eastern end of the Glen Coe area.

3·10

BEN NEVIS

Ben Nevis (affectionately referred to as the 'Ben'), Britain's highest mountain, looks an unspectacular lump from many places, its bulk dominating the town of Fort William and Loch Linnhe. But its huge cliffs, more than 1500 ft (460 m) high, are mainly hidden when the walker is in the town. On sunny and clear days in summer the views over Lochaber and much of the central, western and southern Highlands can be immense. (Note that the Ben has *two* outlier peaks both called Carn Dearg and not to be confused with Carn Mor Dearg.)

SAFETY NOTE

The mountain is ascended by thousands of visitors each year, but it is to be undertaken with care. The general visitor should not tackle it, even by the tourist track, in winter when hours of daylight are limited. More people have been killed on the Ben than have died on the North Face of the Eiger. If the hill is snow-plastered, it should be left to the experienced climber with axe and crampons. The ascent of Ben Nevis, which includes Carn Mar Dearg is for the experienced mountaineer, and should be avoided in winter when there is limited daylight.

Some groups climb the Ben by way of the northern side, following the line of the Allt a' Mhuilinn burn above Fort William golf course to the CIC hut and then on to the arête, but this route is very eroded in sections and some people find the climb to the arête hard and tricky. A direct ascent (and descent) can be made on the southern face, from the car-park at the head of Glen Nevis, but this route is highly dangerous and is for none but the most experienced.

ROUTE DESCRIPTION (Map 13)

The road to Achintee from Claggan passes the town park just past the houses, the site of the annual Ben Nevis race *(1)* to the summit and back. On the R is the Roaring Mill in the River Nevis, a series of pools and cascades, popular with bathers and fishermen. A good path starts from Achintee. Cross a stile and the path leads round the shoulder of Meall an t-Suidhe *(2)* and the upper reaches of Glen Nevis come into sight *(3)*. At about

STARTING AND FINISHING POINT Achintee Farm car-park on the minor road which leads from the Claggan area of Fort William (41-125731). Claggan village lies to the north-west of Fort William on the north bank of the River Nevis. The road to Achintee passes through it and runs alongside the river. The farm is ¾ mile (1.2 km) south-east of the A82.

LENGTH
12 miles (19 km)

ASCENT
4400 ft (1340 m)

500 ft (150 m) a junction path from the Glen Nevis Youth Hostel comes in on your R.

This path forms part of a specially constructed pony trail to a weather observatory which was sited on the top of Ben Nevis last century (4). It was also used in a pioneering motoring bid in which a Model T Ford was driven to the summit (5). The modern paths, both the main route and the junction path from the Youth Hostel, are now very eroded and repair work has been carried out in modern times. You pass the first zig-zags and cross two aluminium bridges constructed by the Lochaber mountain-rescue team and at about 1200 ft (370 m) the path turns north and climbs up a steep score, or gully, in which there are some rowans and birches.

Walkers going straight to the summit by the main track should simply continue uphill on the tourist track and will soon reach the half-way mark at the Red Burn. Care is needed when the path zig-zags near the precipice. Those taking the following route, intended for those who are nimble on the hill, should continue round to the L by the Lochan Meal an t-Suidhe (6). The lochan is a good spot for a rest. To get into Coire Leis go L on a boggy path which descends a little and then runs north for about ½ mile (800 m) and then curves round to the R, west, and eventually south-east.

The Allt a' Mhuilin ('burn of the mill') is on your L and runs up into the corrie. The ground is often boggy and you pick up the remains of an old deer fence. A path and eroded ground take you round to the CIC hut (7), about 1¼ miles (2 km) from Lochan Meall an t-Suidhe. Cross to the other (east) side of the corrie and steep, rocky and scree-strewn slopes take you to the top of Carn Mor Dearg. The going is rough and the rocks are often loose, but a careful way can be picked to the top (8).

Continue on the obvious arête (ridge), which links with the summit slopes of Ben Nevis, proceeding south and then south-west. The distance is under a mile (1.6 km), but care and time are needed because some rock scrambling is involved and sections of the arête seem narrow to the inexperienced and the pull up the final slopes of the Ben can be tiring. The summit is unmistakable, with the Observatory ruins (9) and the Ordnance Survey obelisk. The views can be spectacular.

If you have ascended the whole way by the main tourist track and are tempted to continue to Carn Mor Dearg by descending to the arête, don't unless the day is clear and fine and you know what you are about. There have been several accidents here, including five deaths in one incident, and warning poles have

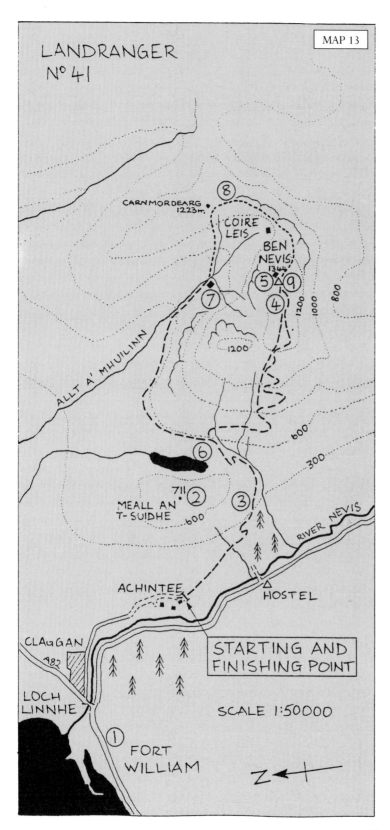

LANDRANGER
Nº 41

MAP 13

CARNMORDEARG
1223m.

COIRE
LEIS

BEN
NEVIS
1344

⑤ △ ⑨

④

⑧

⑦

1200

1000

800

ALLT A' MHUILINN

1200

600

300

⑥

711
MEALL AN
T-SUIDHE ② 600

③

RIVER NEVIS

ACHINTEE

HOSTEL

STARTING AND
FINISHING POINT

CLAGGAN
982

LOCH
LINNHE

① FORT
WILLIAM

SCALE 1:50000

Z ←

65

been erected. Take care, too, on the edges of the plateau, particularly if snow is still around. The summit plateau stretches to about 90 acres (36.5 hectares), but take care on the edges. As you leave the Observatory ruins and the OS indicator you pass quite close to the brink of the cliffs of the north face. The path here is safe, but exercise caution nonetheless.

To descend, pick up the zig-zags of the well-cairned tourist track to the west of the summit and follow these down to the junction at Lochan Meall an t-Suidhe. Look out for a 'well' at about 3500 ft (1070 m) which emerges from beneath the stones. It is known as Buchan's Well and is named after a former secretary of the Scottish Meteorological Society.

1 *Ben Nevis Race*

This famous race, regarded as one of the hardest in Britain, began in 1895, and there are accounts from before it reached its current formalized state, of young and old clocking up some remarkable times. A Mr D. Forbes, of Fort William, reached the summit in three hours and danced a Highland fling on the roof of the observatory there. He was 80. The race was discontinued when the observatory closed in 1904 and also perhaps because in 1903 a contestant had collapsed and remained unconscious for ten hours.

In 1937 the race began again but was temporarily halted once more when World War II broke out. It was resumed in 1943. The number of runners has now soared to more than 500 and the event is still sometimes hit by fierce summit weather. Dave Cannon, of Kendal Athletic Club, won five times in the 1970s and clocked 1 hour 26 minutes and 55 seconds. Women were first officially accepted in 1981. The race is normally held on the first Saturday in September.

2 *Meall an t-Suidhe*

The name of this hill (pronounced *mowl-an-tee*) is translated as 'the moundy hill of the seat'. Above it and the lochan (small loch) of the same name is the half-way point on the tourist track. Just beyond, there was a hut where walkers were charged one shilling for a ticket entitling them to walk to the top. When they got there, they had their ticket stamped with the words 'Ben Nevis Summit'. The receipts were used to keep the path in good condition.

3 *Glen Nevis*

An old tradition has it that the Camerons of Glen Nevis held their lands by the tenure of an unfailing snowball when demanded. There is a similar Highland tradition about the

MacIntyres of Glen Noe, Argyll, and Ben Cruachan, the Munros of Foulis and Ben Wyvis, and the Grants of Rothiemurchus and the Cairngorms. Deep pockets of snow, of course, lie on Ben Nevis all year round and in past times they were dug out for curing fish and taken down in panniers by horses.

Glen Nevis is a beautiful glen and was once the home of the MacSorleys and MacMillans, as well as the Camerons. The striking gorge at its head, which leads through to the grassy meadows at Steall (pronounced *stowl*) was the subject of a public outcry when the North of Scotland Hydroelectricity Board earmarked it for a dam. The scheme was later shelved but could be resurrected.

Ben Nevis from Corpach

4 *Observatory*

The meteorological observatory and hotel were built on the summit last century. The observatory was proposed in 1877 by Mr Milne Home, chairman of the Scottish Meteorological Society, but before it was built readings were first taken in 1881 by the scientist Clement L. Wragge, who later became Government Meteorlogist for Queensland, Australia.

The first observatory was a sheet of tarpaulin covering a stone hut and then a proper building was erected, with sleeping and cooking facilities, and was operated for twenty-one years. It was the first mountain-top observatory in Europe and was officially opened on 17 October 1883. It was linked by phone and telegraph to the post office at Fort William and a hotelier of that town later built a wooden 'hotel' nearby for walkers who wanted to see the sun rise.

5 *Lochan Meall an t-Suidhe*

See note 2. Coire Leis (pronounced *'laish'*) means 'the corrie (hollow) of the sheltered place'.

6 *The CIC Hut*

This Alpine-style, small, stone building at 2200 ft (670 m) is not an open hostel and is owned by the Scottish Mountaineering Club. Dr and Mrs William Inglis Clark donated the hut in memory of their son, Captain Charles Inglis Clark, himself a climber of note, who was killed in World War I. The hut was opened in 1929.

A hut dinner was held to celebrate the opening and the blessing was given by the Rev. A. E. Robertson, the first man to climb all the 'Munros'. Mr Robertson prayed the building might be a refuge to those in need. He had a dramatic response. In burst two climbers who had fallen 600 ft (180 m) down Observatory Gully, shaken and bruised.

67

7 *The Nevis Cliffs*

The main climbs on this north-east face of the Ben, when seen from the slopes of Carn Mor Dearg, include (from the right), the prow of Castle Ridge and the buttresses and gullies of the Castles. Then comes the summit of Carn Dearg itself which is flanked to its left by a wide gully, Moonlight Gully. A three-pronged buttress (L) is known as the Trident and it, in turn, is flanked by two gullies near the line of the summit plateau, No. 4 Gully and No. 3 Gully. Then comes the long line of Tower Ridge running from the plateau down into the corrie and then the on-facing North-east Ridge which is flanked to its left by Observatory Ridge and the arête. All of these features are interspersed by rock, snow and ice climbs of all grades.

8 *The summit*

There has been controversy in modern times over the true height of the Ben and 4418 ft (1350 m) has been given. This includes the OS obelisk, and so the true height is 12 ft (3.7 m) less. The Ben is very busy in season and the monuments on top include memorials to the dead of two world wars and the victims of Hiroshima.

Ben Wyvis and the Cairngorms, to the north-north-east and the east, are almost 60 miles (95 km) away, but can be picked out, as can nearer peaks such as Schiehallion at Loch Rannoch, Ben More and Stobinian at Crianlarich, Buachaille Etive Mor in Glen Coe, Beinn Laoigh (Lui) at Tyndrum, and the Arrochar hills. Southwards and westwards one can see the islands, Arran and Jura, Colonsay, Lismore and Mull and far-off Coll and Tiree. Further still are Barra and South Uist in the Outer Hebrides, over 90 miles (145 km) away and these are seen beyond the smaller Rum, Eigg and Canna.

The Cuillin of Skye can also be seen beyond the hills known as the Streaps, near Loch Arkaig, and to the north-west are Ben Sgriol, across from Knoydart, the Kintail Hills, Torridon, and those fine hills above Glen Affric, Mam Sodhail and Carn Eige. On very clear days the line of the sea can be seen beyond Jura and sometimes a far, low line of land can be picked out: the coast of Northern Ireland, over 120 miles (195 km) away. Nearer at hand, lie the hills, glens and lochs of Lochaber and the Mamores just across the glen.

3·11

THE TOLMOUNT AND JOCK'S ROAD

This historic hill crossing leads from Glen Clova into Glen Doll and crosses a plateau of high hills. It is a walk of contrasts: green Glen Clova and dark Glen Doll, the tiny path leading uphill beside a hill burn to the plateau; big, near-featureless hills and magnificent views; and then a steep drop down to Loch Callater and an onwards, straightforward walk to the A93 in Glen Clunie, and on into Braemar.

SAFETY NOTE

This is a walk to be undertaken with care, with full hill gear, a map and a compass and the ability to use both. It is one of the most evocative hill passes in Scotland, but it is not to be trifled with.

ACCESS

To get to the head of Glen Clova, drive on the B965 from Kirriemuir in Angus, and follow the line of the glen on the west side until you reach the inn at Clova, where there is a bridge over the River South Esk. Continue westwards on a smaller road for 2¼ miles (3.5 km) until you reach the road-end near Braedownie (pronounced *Braedoonie*) farm. There is some parking space in a quarry on the R (north) side of the road at the foot of Red Craig and an official Forestry Commission site further on.

STARTING AND FINISHING POINT The foot of Red Craig, on the north side of the road at Braedownie Farm, Glen Clova (44-288757), Angus.

FINISHING POINT Auchallater Farm, 1¾ miles (3 km) south of Braemar on the A93 (43-155884).

LENGTH 13 miles (21 km)

ASCENT 3000 ft (900 m) at the crest of the pass.

ROUTE DESCRIPTION (Maps 14, 15)

The start of the Jock's Road and Tolmount walk is signposted, as is another pass which comes in from the north near Braedownie, the Capel Mount *(1)* leading to Ballater.

Walk along the road past Glen Doll Youth Hostel and continue on an estate track and path through forestry plantations. Be sure to stay on the R (north) side of the burn, as it is tempting at one stage to go southwards at a junction. The path becomes clearer as it continues westwards and upwards through the trees, some of them showing the result of storms of past years, until it emerges on the open hillside, surrounded by steep and rocky hills. The White Water burn is prominent ahead and on the L, and the path starts to go steeply uphill on the R. This uphill section in Glen Doll is the true Jock's Road *(2)*. Keep going uphill and watch out on the L for a tiny mountain shelter not far from the head of the pass, just to the west of Cairn Lunkard and known as Dave's Bourach *(3)*.

Nearby and on the R of the path is a plaque on a boulder commemorating five hillwalkers who died in storms on the plateau at New Year 1959 *(4)*. The path proceeds north-west with the Munro–top of Tom Buidhe on the L, the Tolmount peak half–L ahead and Cairn Bannoch and its outliers to the R. This is the crux of the pass. Some walkers make deviations to walk to the summit of one or all of these hills and then return to the pass route. If you do deviate, make sure that you have plenty of time. There is a gradual climb to the summit of the pass at 3,000 ft (900 m).

It is easy to lose the path on this part of the crossing and on the central plateau it is often non-existent, but the positions of Tolmount and Tom Buidhe provide an excellent guide to the route. Keep the burn on the east side of Tom Buidhe to your L and proceed over the mound known as Crow Craigies.

From the summit of the pass you can look to the main Cairngorms plateau, north-eastwards over Broad Cairn towards the royal mountain of Lochnagar, and south-westwards to the hills around Glen Shee.

The Tolmount itself shields the steep head of Glen Callater and the path swings westwards below the Knaps of Fafernie and Creag Leachdach, passing through a shallow dip and beside an old fence, and goes steeply down into Coire Breac (not on the map).

The descent to the east of lonely Loch Kander and the Kander Corrie is steep and broken up and you come across the remains of old fence poles. But Loch Callater ahead is an excellent marker and a small burn is picked up, the path going down its east bank and past some shieling ruins *(5)*. Some of the ground is boggy. Continue on the east side of the loch. If by some chance you cross the burn, the Allt an Loch, to the west side there is also a broad track down that side of the loch to its northern end, where there is a lodge. This broad estate-road running down Glen Callater and below Creag Phadruig *(6)* reaches the A93 at Auchallater in Glen Clunie. There is room for parking there, but some walkers prefer to walk another 1¾ miles (3 km) into Braemar. Be careful of traffic and walk on the R-hand side of the road, facing oncoming vehicles.

Opposite Jock's Road looking towards Glen Doll

70

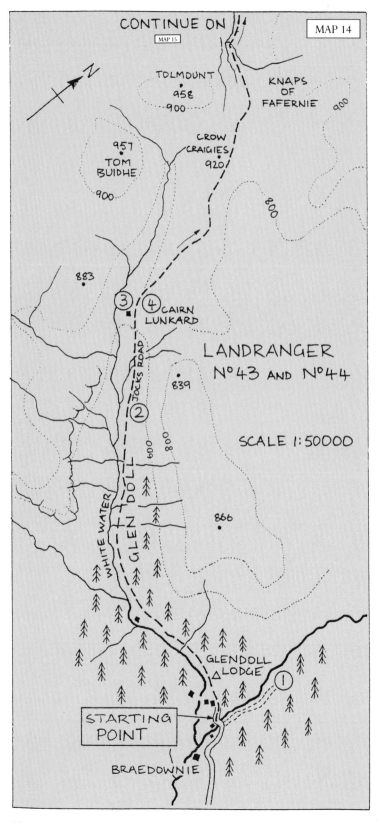

1 *The Tolmount*

This truly historic pass includes Jock's Road and connects *Looking towards Cairn Lunkard* Glen Clova with Deeside. It is one of several of similar character in this area. The old name of the Grampians was the Mounth, which derived from the Gaelic *monadh,* meaning a mountain area or high moorland. The old name for the Cairngorms was the Monadh Rhuadh ('red') and we still have the Monadh Liath ('grey').

The word was corrupted to the Mounth and later came to be applied to individual hill passes and to describe the hill ground as a whole between Upper Deeside and the low ground of Perthshire and west Angus. The correct name of the pass which includes Jock's Road is the Tolmount or Tolmounth. 'Tol' probably derives from a Gaelic word *dail*, meaning a meadow or flat place, as around Braedownie and in fertile Glen Clova.

2 *Jock's Road*

This Glen Doll pass is a right-of-way and was the subject of a a much-publicized nineteenth-century court case. In 1888 a Scot called Duncan Macpherson, who had made his wealth in Australia, bought the Glen Doll estate and tried to close it to the public. The Scottish Rights of Way Society fought him and won, proving that the pass had been a 'trade route' over the years.

The case ultimately went to the House of Lords. A witness and shepherd called James Winter, from Braedownie, said in evidence that the name Jock's Road derived from a land dispute between two owners, Lord Aberdeen and Lord Invercauld. The witness said he was descended from one John Winter, who was allegedly involved with others in

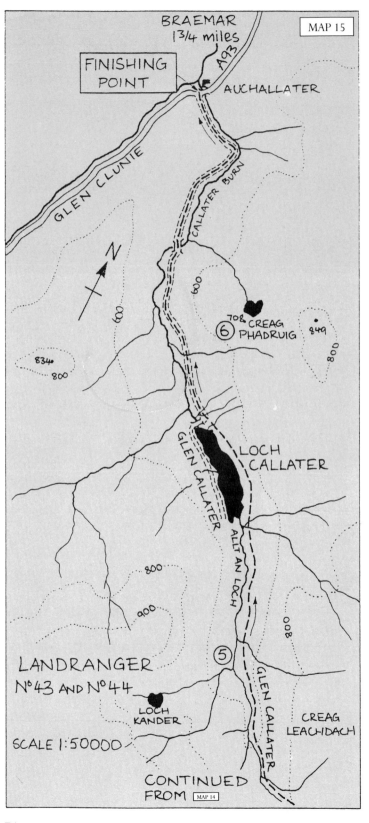

MAP 15

BRAEMAR
1 3/4 miles

A93

FINISHING
POINT

AUCHALLATER

GLEN CLUNIE

CALLATER BURN

N

600

600

708 CREAG
⑥ PHADRUIG

849

800

834
800

LOCH
CALLATER

GLEN CALLATER

ALLT AN LOCH

800

900

800

⑤

LANDRANGER
Nº 43 AND Nº 44

GLEN CALLATER

LOCH
KANDER

CREAG
LEACHDACH

SCALE 1:50000

CONTINUED
FROM MAP 14

forcing Lord Aberdeen to turn back when they met him on the track. Lord Aberdeen was incensed and offered a reward for anyone who could name the ringleader. John Winter felt it prudent to take refuge for some time at the top of Glen Doll in a shepherd's hut and that, said James Winter, was the derivation of Jock's Road.

3 *Mountain shelter*

This little stone hut to the L of the path is informally called Dave's Bourach after Davy Glen, a modern man-of-the-road, and it may be on the site of the original Jock's refuge.

4 *The plaque*

If you walk this pass on a sunny and clear day, it is all too easy to scoff at the mention of safety. But it is a different matter when the plateau is shrouded in mist or plastered in soft and deep snow, and gales are battering the energy from you. The walkers commemorated by the plaque were from Glasgow Universal Hiking Club and included highly experienced people. They were travelling from Braemar to Glen Doll and lost their way in stormy weather on the plateau between the Tolmount and the start of the Jock's Road section. One body was found a few hundred yards from this shelter, then a mainly wooden hut. Some bodies were not found until weeks later. Another couple died in similar storms in March 1976.

5 *Shielings*

The Gaelic people in past centuries left their homes in late spring and headed with their cattle and goats for the fresh grass of the upper glens and moors. They lived in makeshift huts called shielings and returned to the lower ground at the end of summer.

6 *Creag Phadruig*

This crag and a loch nearby take their name from a legendary priest called Patrick (whose name is also commemorated in Carn an t-Sagairt Mor (pronounced *Carn Tagart More*), a peak on the route from Loch Callater to the royal mountain of Lochnagar. (Earmark both Carn an t-Sagairt Mor and Lochnagar for another expedition.) A local tradition has it that when the district experienced what seemed like everlasting frosts they called on Patrick for help. He went to a holy well near Loch Callater and prayed until the ice melted. Rain clouds gathered over Carn an t-Sagairt Mor and the thaw began. The old Gaelic people have nearly all gone from these areas but their names and legends still linger in these hills and add to their charm.

4·12

THE LAIRIG GHRU

STARTING POINT
Entrance gate to
Glen Lui, ¼ mile
(400 m) east of
Linn of Dee and on
the left of the
minor road which
runs westwards for
5 miles (8 km) from
Braemar (off A93)
and then curves
eastwards across
the River Dee at
Linn of Dee (43-
068899).

FINISHING
POINT
Coylum Bridge
village on the A951,
2 miles (3 km) from
Aviemore (A9) (35-
918107)

LENGTH
17 miles (27 km)

ASCENT
2750 ft (840 m) at
the crest of the
pass.

The spectacular gash of the Lairig Ghru through the Cairngorms plateau is a route of great antiquity, packed with legend, an evocative introduction to the area, and one of the best cross-country treks in Scotland.

The crossing is made by thousands each year and sections of the path are now eroded. It is a very old right-of-way and was once much used by the people of Mar and Upper Strathspey.

SAFETY NOTE
Full hill gear should be carried: people have died in this pass and particular care is needed in spring and winter.

ROUTE DESCRIPTION (Maps 16–19)

There is parking space on the L of the road at Linn of Dee and just before the entrance to Glen Lui. The Water of Lui burn is on your R as you pass through a gate on your L on to a broad, stony track. Proceed on this for just over a mile (1.6 km) and as you clear a wood there is a bridge across Lui Water *(1)*. Continue north-west on this track for another 1½ miles (2.5 km) until you reach a boarded-up (at the time of writing) house (R), called Derry Lodge *(2)*. Go past the lodge and through the trees until the ground is more open. Another glen, Glen Derry, and its burn, comes in from the north (R) and on your L is another cottage, Luibeg *(3)*. The Lairig Ghru is signposted at this point and you cross the Derry burn by a bridge and proceed westwards into Glen Luibeg and through groves of attractive pine trees.

About ½ mile (800 m) to the west of Derry Lodge the large track ends just clear of the trees and a path is picked up. A copse of trees here is known as Preas nam Meirleach, the Robbers' Copse *(4)*. The path is then crossed by another burn coming in from the north, the Luibeg burn, and you can either wade it at this point or, if the water is high, go up the east bank of the burn for under ¼ mile (400 m), to a bridge.

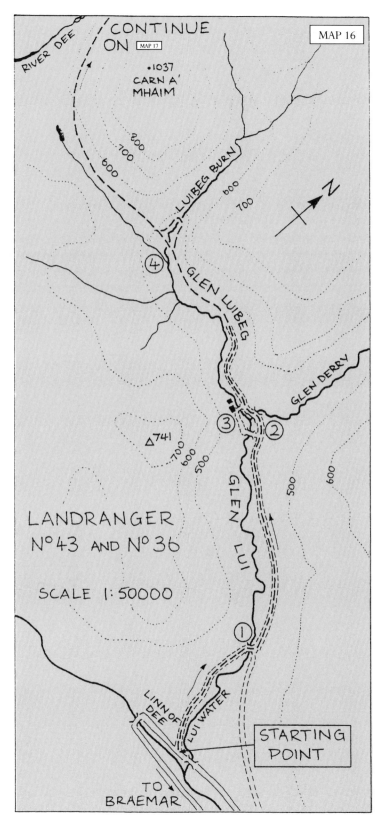

MAP 16

CONTINUE ON MAP 17

RIVER DEE

•1037
CARN A'
MHAIM

800
700
600

LUIBEG BURN

600

700

N

④

GLEN LUIBEG

GLEN DERRY

③ ②

△741

700
600
500

500

600

GLEN LUI

LANDRANGER
N°43 AND N°36

SCALE 1:50000

①

LINN OF DEE

LUI WATER

STARTING
POINT

TO
BRAEMAR

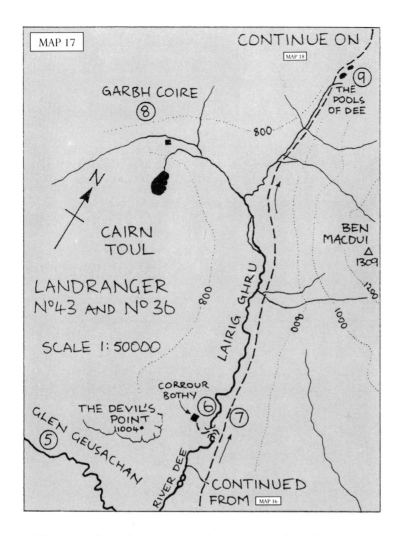

MAP 17

CONTINUE ON

MAP 18

GARBH COIRE
⑧

THE
POOLS
OF DEE
⑨

800

N

CAIRN
TOUL

BEN
MACDUI
△
1309

LANDRANGER
N°43 AND N°36

800

LAIRIG GHRU

1280

SCALE 1:50000

800

1000

CORROUR
BOTHY
⑥

THE DEVIL'S
POINT
1004•

⑦

GLEN GEUSACHAN

⑤

RIVER DEE

CONTINUED
FROM MAP 16

Turn southwards again to the main track and continue westwards for 2 miles (3 km). Curve north-westwards and then north, on a clear path into Glen Dee, the wide glen of the River Dee. You pass below Carn a' Mhaim (R) and there should be good views to the steep, rocky slabs of The Devil's Point (5), half-L ahead, and attractive Glen Geusachan on your L. You are now into the main line of the Lairig Ghru and on the L (west) side of the path and on the L (west) bank of the River Dee you should see a small, stone bothy with a 'tin' roof. This is the famous Corrour Bothy, a much-loved place in Cairngorms lore (6). A very eroded path leads down to a bridge and an even more eroded one to the bothy itself, which is spartan and unlocked. It is a good place for a halt or a refuge in bad weather.

Return to the path and after about ¼ mile (400 m) look out for a large boulder at the R side of the path. This is Clach nan Tailer ('the stone of the tailors') (7) which figured in a Cairngorms story of hill storms and tragedy. Continue

Opposite *Looking across Loch Morloch towards Lairig Ghru and the Cairngorm range*

79

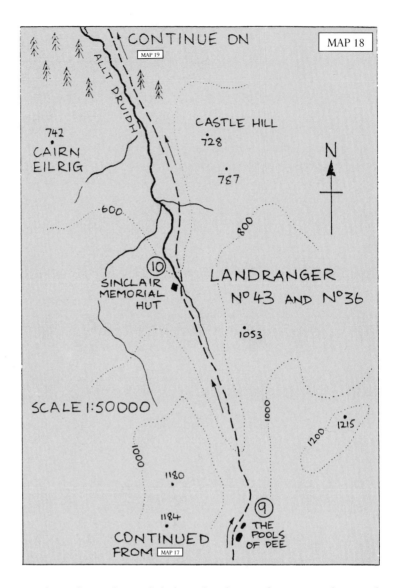

CONTINUE ON MAP 19

MAP 18

742
CAIRN
EILRIG

ALLT DRUIDH

CASTLE HILL
728

787

N

600

800

SINCLAIR
MEMORIAL
HUT

LANDRANGER
Nº 43 AND Nº 36

1053

SCALE 1:50000

1000

1200 1215

1000

1180

1184

CONTINUED
FROM MAP 17

THE
POOLS
OF DEE

northwards on the path below the slopes of Cairn Toul (L) and Ben Macdui (R) and look out on your L for the magnificent Garbh Coire ('the rough corrie') *(8)*. The path becomes increasingly stony and begins to rise to its crest. Boulder fields make for some awkward walking, particularly in new snow, and 3 miles (5 km) from Corrour the crest is reached and marked by small lochans, the Pools of Dee *(9)*. Continue to the L of these. The boulder fields continue for about a mile (1.6 km) and the track is sometimes lost among them.

The route goes downhill and passes below Creag an Leth-Choin (Lurcher's Crag). About 2½ miles (4 km) from the Pools of Dee another junction path goes off R (north-east) to Glen More and the foot of Cairngorm. Continue downhill on the R (east) bank of the burn and you pass a modern building, the

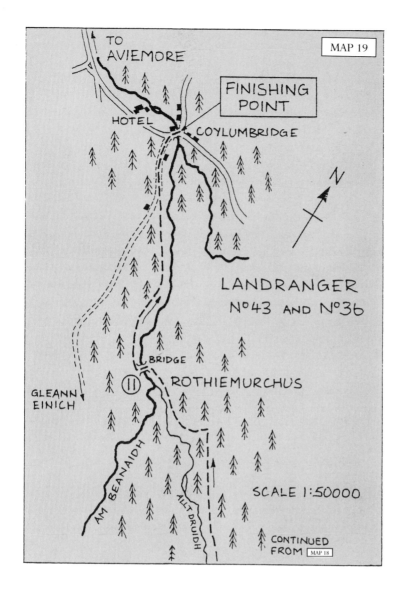

MAP 19

TO AVIEMORE

FINISHING POINT

HOTEL

COYLUMBRIDGE

N

LANDRANGER N°43 AND N°36

BRIDGE

GLEANN EINICH

⑪ ROTHIEMURCHUS

AM BEANAIDH

ALLT DRUIDH

SCALE 1:50000

CONTINUED FROM MAP 18

Sinclair Memorial Hut *(10)* (L) on the other bank. Stay on the R (east) side of the burn, the Allt Druidh, as you descend. The path downhill reaches the lovely woods of Rothiemurchus south of this hut and you pass between the lower slopes of Cairn Eilrig (L) and Castle Hill on your R (east). Ignore a junction path going right (east). Descend steeply on a good path through these attractive woods for another mile (1.6 km) until you come to a path junction. Go L (west).

After 1¼ miles (2 km) you reach the Cairngorm Club's footbridge *(11)* across the now-enlarged Alt Druidh burn which has been joined by the Am Beanaidh from the south. Just after the footbridge you come to another junction path coming in from the L (west). Continue straight on downhill and about 1½ miles (2.5 km) from the bridge another junction path comes in from the south, down from Gleann Einich. Continue northwards through trees for another ½ mile (800 m) and you reach the road near a caravan park at Coylum Bridge, where there is a hotel ¼ mile (400 m) L (west).

1 *Lui Water*

The name 'Lui' derives from the Gaelic *laoigh*, a calf, and in most cases where it occurs means a deer calf. Another famous Cairngorm pass, the Lairig an Laoigh, links with the Lairig Ghru just past Derry Lodge and in past times cattle were often driven through it. Cattle and sheep were driven through the Lairig Ghru, too, and Highland girls once walked through the pass in summer carrying baskets of eggs on their heads.

2 *Derry Lodge*

This building is a relic of the heyday of stag shooting. The name derives from the Gaelic *doire*, meaning a grove or clump of trees. That peerless naturalist, piper, hillwalker and writer Seton Gordon, who died in 1977, recalled playing golf in the clearing between the trees at Derry Lodge with a famous stalker, old Donald Fraser, but all traces of the home-made 'course' have now gone.

3 *Luibeg*

This name means 'the little calf'. The keeper's house here is one of the few remaining buildings in a glen and strath which once held dozens of houses. The ruins or foundations of some can be seen on the left beside the track between Linn of Dee and Derry Lodge. Some of those expelled to make way for the big sporting estates of the nineteenth century were the descendants of people who had fought on the Jacobite side in the 1715 rising and some of them were evicted not long after that time. The two main passes of the Cairngorms diverge at this point, the Lairig Laoigh going north by Glen Derry, the Lairig Ghru west by Glen Luibeg.

4 *Preas nam Meirleach*

This grove of trees on the outermost fringe of the pines as you proceed westwards is reputed to be a place where cattle raiders from Lochaber hid from possible pursuit. A burn of that name joins the Luibeg burn just over a mile (1.6 km) to the west of Derry Lodge. The path passes below a hill site which has a legend of buried treasure attached to it, Coire Craobh an Oir, on the hill called Carn Crom.

The hill's name means a twist or bend and a coire (corrie)

is a saucer- or bowl-shaped depression in the hills (long ago, the word meant a kettle or cauldron).

The woods of Rothiemurchus near the Cairngorms Club's footbridge

5 *The Devil's Point*

This name is a polite or coy interpretation of the original Gaelic name Bon au Deamhain (pronounced *Pote an dyaw-in*), 'the Devil's penis'. Nearly all Gaelic names are descriptive and often give valuable information about the state of the ground. At this point you are passing below the slopes of Carn a' Mhaim (the last word is pronounced *vane*), 'the middle cairn', and looking across to the mass of Beinn Bhrotain (pronounced *pain vroetan*).

This hill derives its name from Brodan, the dog of Fingal, the hero-king of Gaelic mythology (although he may have had a factual basis). There are good views into magnificent Glen Geusachan, 'the glen of the little pine wood'. The name derives from Giubhsachain (pronounced *gyoosachan*). The pines have now gone and only stumps remain, but one of the joys of the Lairig Ghru crossing is that it gives such good views to so many striking mountains and big corries which can be borne in mind for the future.

6 *Corrour Bothy*

This is perhaps the most famous mountain shelter in the Cairngorms. The name derives from the wide Coire Odhar (pronounced *Corrie Ower*), 'dun-coloured corrie', which runs from behind the bothy on Devil's Point round to Cairn Toul. A stalker's path goes up the corrie from the bothy, a pleasant means of ascent to both hills, but it should be noted that it is a perilous corner in winter and should not be undertaken then except by experienced and adequately equipped mountaineers.

The bothy dates back to 1877 and was well used in the heyday of Victorian and Edwardian shooting. It later fell into disuse, but was still widely used as a haven or base for hill expeditions. The Cairngorm Club and other enthusiasts were responsible for its renovation in 1950 and for erecting the bridge.

7 *Clach nan Tailer*

This flat stone with ribbed lines tells an old tale of a wager that ended in disaster. The tailors made a bet one Hogmanay that they would dance at three 'dells' within twenty-four hours. 'Dell' is a corruption of the Gaelic word *dail*, a meadow or flat place, from which the place-name Dal comes. They successfully danced at Abernethy and Rothiemurchus and then set out through the Lairig for Dalmore, at the site of present-day Mar Lodge. The pass is a dangerous place in winter and they were overtaken by a blizzard and died while taking shelter in the lee of the stone that now bears their name.

8 *Garbh Coire*

This big corrie to the left (west) of the path is believed to be one of the most beautiful in the Cairngorms and is mentioned in one of the songs of the Cairngorms poet William Smith. It forms part of that great mountain, Braeriach (Am Braigh Riabhach, 'the brindled hill'), the second highest in the Cairngorms. It has another corrie leading off from it, Coire Bhrochain ('the corrie of gruel'), a name some think is somewhat fanciful and which is supposed to be derived from the fact of cattle at shieling times falling over the cliffs and being reduced to the consistency of porridge. Seton Gordon sent for analysis some bones found there and one was identified as the jawbone of an ox.

9 *The Pools of Dee*

Keep a look out for ptarmigan, mountain grouse, at the crest of the pass. They are frequently seen and nest there. At the

1912

THIS BRIDGE
OVER THE ALLT NA BEINNE MOIRE
LARIG GHRU ROUTE
WAS ERECTED BY
THE CAIRNGORM CLUB ABERDEEN
THROUGH ITS COMMITTEE
WITH THE ASSISTANCE OF
MANY MOUNTAIN-LOVING FRIENDS.

T.R.GILLIES   JOHN CLARKE
TREASURER.   CHAIRMAN.

The Cairngorm Club footbridge

summit of the pass the Allt na Criche, 'March burn', comes down from the plateau and disappears underground in the boulder fields, to reappear on the Dee side of the summit as one large and three smaller pools. Trout can be seen. The old name was Lochan Dubh na Lairige, 'the small black loch of the lairig'.

10 *The Sinclair Memorial Hut*

This building is Spartan in appearance and the path around it is very eroded. It commemorates Lieutenant-Colonel W. A. Sinclair, who died in these hills in 1954, and was opened in 1957. It arouses strong feelings among Cairngorms enthusiasts who feel that new buildings should not be erected.

11 *Cairngorm Club footbridge*

The Cairngorm Club is the oldest mountaineering club in Scotland. A group of Aberdeen hillwalkers decided to celebrate Queen Victoria's Golden Jubilee on 22 June 1887 by setting off rockets and fireworks on the summit of Ben Macdui. The six founder-members went to the Shelter Stone, on the shores of Loch Avon, spent the night there and the next day, on the shores of the loch, decided to form the Cairngorm Club for 'men and women of heroic spirit, and possessed of souls open to the influence and enjoyment of nature pure and simple as displayed among our loftiest mountains'. The club's formal constitution was drawn up in Aberdeen on 9 January 1889.

SELECTED WALKS IN THE NORTH-WEST HIGHLANDS AND ISLANDS

Hamish Brown

Highland Cattle

INTRODUCTION

The Great Glen, Glen Alba, that great geographical tear-fault with Loch Ness and the Caledonian Canal filling it (from Fort William to Inverness) is a psychological as well as a physical landmark. Improved roads and more reliable cars have made it much easier to reach, yet somehow, even to walkers living in the Scottish Lowlands, never mind south of the border, there is an aura of remoteness, toughness and other-worldliness about the lands 'beyond the Great Glen'. Hopefully, the six, very varied, walks described here will lure the curious traveller into that magical region.

Magical it is, as if the Creator, having worked up through the land, suddenly began to be more lavish in his use of the spectacular. The Outer Hebrides of course believe they are God's jewels, scattered before He sat back on the Seventh Day. The beauty has a diamond hardness about it. This is Kipling's 'edge of cultivation'. Man hangs on with a limpet's tenacity here, where there are some of the oldest rocks in the world. Glaciers have cut deep into the mountains, and the vegetation is as thin as a scarecrow's coat. Sea and sky are like living beasts, pawing and knawing at the land. Beyond the Great Glen the landscape goes into overdrive and, for the walker new to it, the experience can be a bit breathless.

To select just six walks from this wealth is like asking a botanist to pick six flowers from the flora of the British Isles. A score of islands and a hundred bens and glens spring to mind. Skye, being the Valhalla of the Scottish mountains, chose itself. Everyone, some day, has to discover the Cuillin. Ben More in Mull offers the only other island 'Munro' and is a favourite of many. We must apologize to Shetland, Orkney, the whole Outer Hebrides and a dozen Inner Hebridean islands. Maybe it is as well: islands can be addictive.

Coastal walking in Scotland has hardly been discovered yet so I felt one walk of that type was needed. The Stacks of Duncansby are unforgettable, even if one of the easiest walks in this book.

Beinn a' Bha'ach Ard I include slightly tongue-in-cheek. It is not often climbed, not being a Munro. It is a Corbett however and illustrates the wealth of attractive walking, and superlative summit views, to be had from hills near, yet below, the Plimsoll line of 3000 ft (914 m). Be warned though: Corbetts can also be habit-forming.

The next two routes all offer the option of reaching Munro height within the framework of longer traverses or circuits. Mull and Torridon are notable tourist showplaces but we go behind the scenes. Legs, not wheels, lead to the real perform-ances. And we can write our own script! These can be serious undertakings. 'Take care, or the undertaker does the taking', as one of my mentors cheerfully put it.

In the north-west the extraordinary peaks seem to straggle across the watery world like a herd of petrified mammoths. There had to be something from Assynt and Quinag, a mountain of mountains, is as fine as any. And then there is Skye. Poucher called his book on the island *The Magic of Skye*. Magic it is: Aslan country, not a tame country at all. I trust you are roaring to go!

Loch Torridon

1·13

THE STACKS OF DUNCANSBY

This walk is both short and easy. In this case, though, small is not only beautiful but also spectacular. Were the Stacks of Duncansby sited other than in the extreme north-east corner of Scotland, they would be very well known. John o' Groats, undeniably a tourist attraction, lies only 2 miles (3 km) away as the crow flies, but 90% of tourists never go more than ¼ mile (400 m) from their cars. The Stacks are all ours, serendipity for the walker.

STARTING AND FINISHING POINT John o' Groats at the end of the A9 in Caithness (12-380734). The Ordnance Survey 1:25,000 Pathfinder map ND37/47 gives more names of interest and is useful for showing fences and other details.

LENGTH
6 miles (9 km)

ASCENT
330 ft (100 m)

ROUTE DESCRIPTION (Map 20)

From the harbour *(1)* walk eastwards for ⅝ mile (1 km) between fields and sea with the tidal sands held in place, as it were, by the nails of seaward rocks. Just before Robert's Haven and the bulge of the Ness of Duncansby is the site of an early chapel. Between the Ness (Norse for 'headland') and the Island of Stroma, the sea is often in turmoil: this is the tide-race of the Boars of Duncansby *(2)*. The Bay of Sannick is another sandy shelter, where waders may gather *(3)*. Leave the bay where the burn flows into it, for the character of the walk changes. From now on it is cliff-top walking rather than seaside strolling. The cliff edge is fenced off until nearly opposite the Stacks of Duncansby. For me, Duncansby Head *(4)*, thrusting out into the sea, is the geographical counterpart of Land's End.

Working down southwards, detour round the Geo of Sclaites. From the point of its south side Humlies Hole is a pillar only just connected to the cliff—a stack for the future. There is a cave in the back of the rift and an off-shore stack called The Knee and another, under the cliff, Gibb's Crag.

As you move on, the twin Stacks of Duncansby seem to dodge in and out from the red sandstone cliffs. There are two of these fangs (and the stumps of other molars long ago worn-down to the gums of the sea), rufous and green, vertical rock, vertical vegetation, every horizontal seemingly possessed by birds, from attic fulmars to basement shags. Another prow of

The sands at John o' Groats

cliff is being chiselled off by nature and the Stacks have holes through them. Nothing is still, not even the rock itself *(5)*. The cliffs reach a maximum of 265 ft (81 m) on Hill of Crogodale, ⅓ mile (500 m) south of the Stacks, a good turning point for the walk.

Return by the same route to the hollow below the lighthouse hill, then cut across to pick up the lighthouse road and walk along it into the scattered crofts and houses of John o' Groats. Alternatively aim directly towards the houses, picking up a track off the moors leading into the 'school' shown on maps (i.e. head due north-west from Hill of Crogodale).

1 The Story of John o' Groats
Jan de Groot is buried at Canisbay Church, 2½ miles (4 km) west of John o' Groats. This old Danish (Viking)-influenced church is near the Castle of Mey, the home of the Queen

Mother, who attends services when in the north. The John o' Groats name has a popular derivation but an explanation did not appear in print until the 1791 *Statistical Account*. This tells of three de Groot brothers (of Dutch origins) settling in the area in the fifteenth century. At an annual family gathering a great quarrel arose over precedence and Jan (John) solved this issue by building an octagonal house with eight doors and an octagonal table in the centre so that each son could enter on level terms. The house had gone by the time eighteenth-century travellers arrived but the hotel has re-created this architectural oddity. The most northerly point is Dunnet Head, 11 miles (18 km) west of here, another spectacular

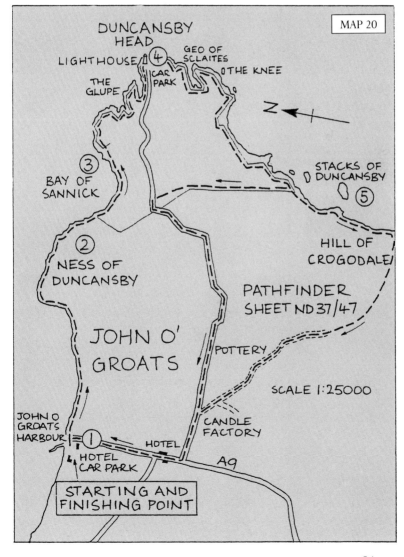

400-ft (120 m) cliff bluff with a lighthouse on top. Timothy Pont, the great cartographer, was minister of Dunnet Kirk.

2 *Duncansby*

This name is older than that of John o' Groats. Duncan (Dungal) was a Celtic *mormaor* (earl) whose name the Norse gave to the district. The first Atlantic chart (1569) has it as Dungesbi. The Head was named on Ptolemy's map, the first-ever (first century AD) map to show Britain.

3 *Bird-life*

Turnstones, purple sandpipers, ringed plovers, and dunlins (red-backed sandpipers) are the commonest shore visitors in winter. Rarer are bar-tailed godwits, knots and sanderlings. Corncrakes are rare now and birds like the snow bunting and redwing are at the southern edge of their northern range. Puffins, guillemots, razorbills, kittiwakes, shags and *tysties* (black guillemots) are some of the cliff nesters, along with pipits and rock doves. Gannets and both great and Arctic skuas can be watched offshore.

On the northern sands you may also find 'groaty buckies', small, pink-tinted cowries, and the only cowrie found in European waters. Seals are common and the area has several stories connected with seals, the *selkies* of the sea, who could take on human form. Eric Linklater's *Sealskin Trousers* is a famous modern story on this old theme.

4 *Duncansby Head*

When I walked from John o' Groats to Land's End, a story told in *Hamish's Groat's End Walk* (Gollancz/Paladin), I began at Duncansby Head, with the Stacks of Duncansby being almost symbols of the journey. Most walkers, rather than Groat's End racers, have expressed the same feelings: Duncansby Head is the worthier starting or finishing point.

5 *The Stacks*

'No traveller, when he comes to John o' Groats, will repent a visit to the Head. The Stalks [*sic*] of Duncansby are two pyramidal-pillars of natural freestone-rock. They rear their fantastic summits a great way into the air and strike the eye as the huge spires of some old, magnificent Gothic pile.' So was the scene described in the 1791 *Statistical Account*. The stacks are locally Muckle (big) Stack and Peedie (small) Stack and there is a much smaller third stack. They are made of old red sandstone, the horizontal strata of which give the stepped-pyramid effect. Sea eagles once nested on their crests.

Opposite *The Stacks of Duncansby*

Beinn a' Bha'ach Ard

STARTING AND
FINISHING POINT
Car-park on the
Glen Strathfarrar
road by Culligran
power station.
(26-378404)
   Use the second
series 1:50,000 map
for accuracy.

LENGTH
7½ miles (12 km)

ASCENT
2900 ft (880 m)

This hill, whose name is pronounced *Ben ah Vaichart,* is a classic example of the good things to be found in the Scottish Highlands without subjecting yourself to the historical tyranny of Munro altitude (3000 ft/914 m). The lower parts are covered in attractive native birch forest and above lie easy heather or grassy slopes leading to a notable view-point, not only of the mountains but of the lowland country round the Moray Firth. This is a walk for a clear day in early summer.

ACCESS
The road from Struy up Glen Strathfarrar is not open freely to vehicular traffic, there being a locked gate at Inchmore (26-396405), but permission/admission can normally be obtained from the house beside the gate. (Check beforehand by telephoning Struy (046376)260.) The hill should not be ascended from mid-August to the third week in October, as this is the deer-stalking season.

ROUTE DESCRIPTION (Map 21)

The entrance to the Culligran power station *(1)* is rather hidden in the trees, but the unsurfaced road that passes it is clear enough. Please do not park on the power-station side of the road; there is plenty of space opposite or near by.

   The road is used by the estate *(2)* as well as providing access for the hydro-electric service. It rises steeply then swings L to wander through some fine birch woods *(3)*. A track bearing off back half-R leads to the top station of the power station's pipeline and shortly after there is another R branch (shown as a footpath on the 1:50,000 map). Ignore these for the main road westwards. Roe-deer can sometimes be seen and in season there are areas of lush blaeberries (bilberries) to excite the taste buds and stain fingers and tongue.

   The wood opens out as the road follows the glen of the Neaty Burn. A power line runs parallel with the road and river, a river

which never flows very full as, ⅝ mile (1 km) along, you find a *Rocks in Glen* small water-intake dam. The water is borrowed for creating *Strathfarrar* power *(4)*. The rough road ends at this point.

There is no path shown on the map but one runs up the east bank of the Neaty Burn from here. It is not a 'made' path but is the result of 'go-anywhere' vehicles carrying down deer from the hill. In less than ⅓ mile (500 m) it reaches the path shown on the map and takes over from what was once a superb stalkers' path from the days when ponies brought down the deer. The old stalkers' path below this level is now completely overgrown and quite impossible to see in places.

Continue up the track on the east bank to the junction with the stream descending directly from Beinn a' Bha'ach Ard, a somewhat damper area, and then closely follow the line of this side stream, the Allt Doire Bhuig ('stream of the damp wood'), on good firm ground. (The track goes on up the glen for another ⅝ mile (1 km) and then swings off uphill to the west.) In June the line of the Allt Doire Bhuig shows a succession of beautiful, and often rare, mountain flowers *(5)*.

The stream is welcome on a hot day, so have a good drink before it peters out. When there is no burn to follow, just head straight up the steep slope northwards to gain the easy west ridge of the hill. This leads gently along to the final cone of the summit bump, where there is an Ordnance Survey obelisk and cairn and a view with a dramatic sweep to the east *(6)*.

Real alternative routes off the hill are not practical, but the west ridge could be followed to the Neaty Burn or the ups and downs of the craggier south ridge could be followed as long as the heather remains close cropped and easy to walk on. Head

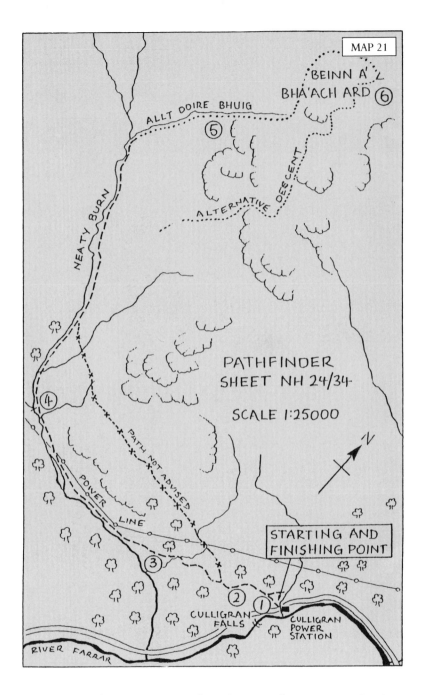

MAP 21

down to the Neaty Burn when the going becomes rougher but be careful in working through the minor crags.

The return by the Neaty Burn and the hydro road is no dull repetition but rewards the walker with changing views and wildlife. Few good summits can be scaled so easily or give such a sample of the true variety of Highland scenery. Though not a Munro, this hill, small by Scottish standards, is still higher than most in England. The summit view emphasizes that.

1 *Culligran Power Station* *Near Culligran*

The power station is actually hidden underground. All we see is the entrance. It is fed by a tunnel from the dammed Loch Beannacharan further up the glen and also by an aqueduct from above Culligran farm which captures all the drainage east of our hill. The Neaty Burn is also tapped. As this is an important salmon river, there is a fish lift at Loch Beannacharan and the Culligran falls have also been made easier for fish to pass. The falls lie ⅓ mile (500 m) up from here and are worth seeing. The rock strata are much folded.

2 *Highland estates*

Red deer were originally forest animals. Being forced by our man-altered landscape to live on the hostile heights, their numbers have to be strictly controlled. Even so, a bad winter or spring can see many die of starvation, a fact overlooked by the sentimental objectors to shooting deer. Remote estates are often the only source of local employment. They have built the paths which we, as walkers, find so useful for our pleasurable pastime.

3 *Birch woods*

Birch woods like this go back to the last Ice Age. Birch is one of the first colonizers of waste ground, river flushes, etc. The trees were often coppiced in olden times. Bundles of birch were laid on the bogs of Rannoch Moor as a base for the railway line.

4 *Borrowed water*

This is an apt description. Loch Monar at the head of Glen Strathfarrar has a huge catchment area, including aqueducts capturing streams well down below the level of its two dams. The water is piped to a power station by Loch Beannacharan and that loch's waters are piped to the Culligran power station (taking in the Neaty Burn *en passant*). The Farrar waters join the much-used Affric-River Glass waters and, on what becomes the River Beauly, there are two dams at Aigas and Kilmorack before the water is returned to flow into the sea. At Aigas one can see the fish lift in operation in the summer months.

5 *Mountain flowers*

I noted cow wheat, cloudberry, tormentil, chickweed-wintergreen, dwarf cornel, lousewort, slender St John's wort, besides ling, both heathers, cotton grass and various attractive mosses.

6 *The summit view*

The Black Isle is really a peninsula between the Beauly Firth and the Cromarty Firth. It dominates the view seaward. There is attractive country between here and Inverness and a glimpse of the distant Cairngorms. To the west and south are a seemingly endless array of mountains, the Lapaichs and Affric hills being the highest hills north of the Great Glen.

3·15

BEN MORE, MULL

Ben More, Skye hills apart, is the highest peak in all the Hebrides and so has a marvellously dominant lordship over the western seaboard. However, don't rush to Mull to climb Ben More only. Enjoy the island and, on some peerless morning, head off up the big hill.

The island setting ensures that the hill is never busy, but it does also occupy a special place for those climbing all the Munros, frequently being kept as the celebratory 'last Munro'. Ben More's tent-shaped crest is instantly recognized from many view-points and it is a bold, rugged hill, giving a grand ascent in keeping with the special nature of the delightful island of Mull. There are also two Corbetts (the listed 2500 ft/762 m summits), so Mull has big hills as well as many hills and offers a great variety of ascents and through routes.

Ben More can be climbed by many different routes, the quickest and easiest being from Dhiseig on Loch na Keal, but such a fine peak deserves a worthy traverse, rather than the easiest option. Ben More or A' Chioch, above the 2000–2300 ft (600–700 m) level, is a mix of scree, rocks and boulders, so be adequately shod for such rough going.

ACCESS
A traverse of the mountain means a transport problem so there has to be a non-climbing driver willing to drop people off and collect them later, or you form two groups walking in opposite directions, or you have two cars. (The price of the ferry encourages you to cross with a full car!) As some such arrangement may not always be possible, alternative circuits, south and north, are also described. The main description is of a south-north traverse, from Glen More to Loch na Keal.

Glen More is really two east-west glens sharing a single name and clearly demarcating Ben More to the south. From Craignure there are 17 miles (27 km) of narrow road to the start. The road swings round (by new plantings) above a chain of lochs to pass a watershed and down into the western part of Glen More. At Craig, the only building in the glen, you have perhaps the finest local view of Ben More. As the glen levels out you reach Teanga Brideig, the starting-point.

This point is easily spotted, as there is a graceful wee bridge (with a

STARTING POINT
Teanga Brideig on A849 in Glen More, 2 miles (3 km) up from Loch Scridain. Parking on old road by bridge (48-564306).

FINISHING POINT
(OR START OF NORTHERN ROUTE)
B8035 along Loch na Keal at the Abhainn na h-Uamha. Roadside parking (48-506367).

LENGTH
7 miles (11 km)

ASCENT
3600 ft (1100 m)

guardian holly tree), part of the older motor road before realignments
were made. Park on the old road, west of the burn.

Deer-stalking takes place from mid-August to near the end of
October. An ascent of Ben More is seldom affected, but check locally
(tel.: Aros (06803) 410). The Bartholomew 1:100,000 map, number
47, is useful as it covers the whole island and its approaches in one
sheet.

ROUTE DESCRIPTION (Map 22)

There is a notice pointing out the route, an old right-of-way,
still a clear path which can be seen curving up the first slopes,
east of the two torrent gashes *(1)*.

The Allt Teanga Brideig is 'stream of St Bride's tongue of
land', Mull having as many saints as castles *(2)*.

The path leads up to a distinctive col. The north side down
into Glen Clachaig is much steeper. The old route descends it to
Loch Ba and the head of Loch na Keal before crossing the 2-
mile (3 km) neck of land to Salen, a fine alternative walk if Ben
More refuses to clear of cloud. The col is not named (it is Mam
Clachaig, 'pass of the stony route'), but the cairn is Carn Cul
Righ Albainn ('cairn with its back on Scotland', traditionally a
boundary mark between Picts and Scots).

Turn west up the ridge, which is simply followed to the top
of A' Chioch *(3)*. The R edge is the scalloped head of Glen
Clachaig, so route-finding is not difficult. The summit is 'a great
heap of rubble' or 'a crumbling ruin', depending on whom you
read. A' Chioch (*c.* 2780 ft, *c.* 850 m) is 'the pap' and back,
across the pass, Cruachan Dearg ('the red peak') is a similar
symmetrical cone. The best of A' Chioch is the view to it from
Ben More, so press on!

A brief bouldery descent leads to the splendid arc of ridge
running to Ben More and bounded by the great northern corrie.
This narrow crest calls for some scrambling but easy options are
always available and it is possible to traverse below the crest on
this south side if it is too intimidating or if a gale is blowing
across the ridge. The scramble along the crest, however, is what
makes this approach memorable. A last flourish (boulders again)
leads to the summit Ordnance Survey obelisk on the stony
plateau and a view which doubles in scale at a stride.

On a clear day the view can extend from Errigal in Ireland to
Ben Nevis, and from the Hebrides to Galloway. Westwards lies
the long arm of land known as the Ross of Mull. Off its
extremity is Iona, the island of St Columba and the burial place

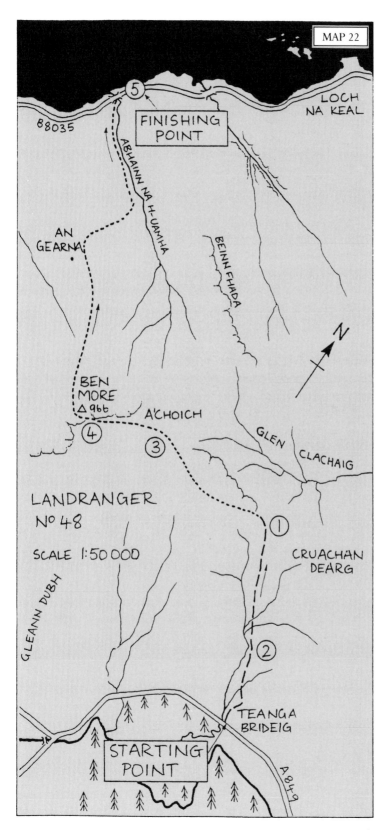

MAP 22

LOCH
NA KEAL

B8035

FINISHING
POINT

ABHAINN NA H-UAMHA

AN
GEARNA

BEINN FHADA

N

BEN
MORE
△ 966   A'CHOICH

④   ③

GLEN
CLACHAIG

LANDRANGER
No 48

①

SCALE 1:50 000

CRUACHAN
DEARG

GLEANN DUBH

②

TEANGA
BRIDEIG

STARTING
POINT

A849

of the early Scottish kings. The island of Erraid is also there, the scene of the shipwreck in R. L. Stevenson's masterpiece *Kidnapped*. The chunky island well out to sea is Staffa, which has Fingal's Cave, with its romantic musical and literary associations. The Cuillin of Rhum and the Cuillin of Skye are arrayed behind the Ardnamurchan peninsula, the most westerly point of mainland Britain. Ulva and the Treshnish Islands lie at the mouth of Loch na Keal. On Mull you have landscape, seascape and cloudscape.

The compass can be completely erratic on top of Ben More *(4)*, so careful navigation is needed in cloud. The great bite of the northern corrie can hardly be missed, however, and following its edge gives help at the start of the descent. There are also cairns marking the route. By the time the dome of An Gearna (with a prominent cairn) is reached, you are usually out of cloud and can descend to Loch na Keal almost anywhere. Dhiseig farmhouse is the *voie normale* but my preference is to swing north-east to join the Abhainn na h-Uamha ('the river of the cave') for this has many fine pools and falls, the former very welcome on a hot day. Where stream meets road is also a clear rendezvous for a driver trying to link up with walkers. There is plenty of roadside parking *(5)*.

If you have to return to the start, the slaggy south ridge can be followed, bearing off to Maol nan Damh ('dome of the hind') and then down Coire nan Each ('horse corrie') and Gleann Dubh ('black glen') to cut round once the lower slopes are reached. Or descend due south to the charming Loch Beg. At low tide you can cross direct (by the marker posts) to the Kinloch Hotel on the south shore. Either way, an hour's walking takes you back to Teanga Brideig.

My recommended circuit from the north would be to wander up Gleann na Beinn Fhada to the col at its head and then ascend A' Chioch's north-east ridge, which will provide 'variety for mind and muscle'. Traverse to and descend Ben More as already described. The traverse of knobbly Beinn Fhada ('long hill'), with a secretive lochan below its summit, is another good start, giving the full circuit of the grander, northern side of Ben More, a round of about 8 miles (13 km) with an ascent of 4250 ft (1300 m).

1 Historic pass

Opposite *Loch Scridain from Am Binnein*

This is the route of an historic drove road (Mull once exported 2000 head of cattle a year), and also the way travellers went before the road round the Gribun was opened

up. The Gribun is quite the most exciting drive on Mull and in wild weather can be dramatic, with waves crashing beside the road and the falls blowing back over the rocky bluffs. The sea was the main highway in Mull in ancient times.

2 *St Bride*

There were several saints called Bride (Brigid or Bridget), the most famous being St Brigid of Kildare. Her saint's day was 12 February and an old Mull proverb said 'On St Bride's day the adder comes out of the hill' (that is, from hibernation). Keep an eye open for these beautiful creatures.

3 *Geology*

Mull's geology is complex but A' Chioch and Ben More are basalt peaks, the eroded, glaciated remnants of a great centre of volcanic activity. At Burgh a fossilized tree stands mute witness to the overwhelming lava flows, once 6000 ft (1830 m) thick and, as Ben More, the most elevated Tertiary basalt in Britain. The columns of basalt at Fingal's Cave on Staffa are world famous. At the end of the Ross of Mull, granite rounds the landscape and Iona is of gneiss, some of the oldest rock in the world. Marble was long quarried on Iona.

4 *Compass errors*

Magnetic anomalies in the Highlands are mostly found in the west. Most people know of the Cuillin summits and crests being badly affected, but there are many other areas where the compass can lead you astray. The northern slopes of Ladhar Bheinn once led me a merry dance in thick cloud and Compass Hill on Canna gives a warning in its name. The deflection seldom lasts long once off summits and crests, but it is leaving those places that most demands navigational accuracy.

5 *Loch na Keal*

Sarah Murray, the pioneering guidebook writer, travelled extensively on Mull in 1800. Along Loch na Keal she described her riding problems: 'In ascending I was obliged to lie on the horse's neck, and in descending almost on his tail, but for all that I could not help gazing at the huge masses of rock piled like folio books one upon another, all the way up the mountain, hanging over my head.' When Lochbuie tried to keep her an extra day at Moy because of the wicked weather, she records that her servant expostulated 'In truth, sir, it can't hurt her, for the rain will only drive on her back.' The trees at the head of Loch na Keal have that rising, planed-off appearance that testifies to strong winds. As locals warn, 'Beware the westerly weather'.

3·16

THE HIDDEN HEART OF TORRIDON

This walk goes into some of the most magnificently wild country in Britain and, apart from the ascent of Ruadh-stac Mor, is on paths, which are rough in places, often 'slaistery' and yielding a loneliness of atmosphere quite unknown in England and seldom equalled in Scotland. The walk round Liathach by itself, on a good day, would be two grades lower, the visit to Coire Mhic Fhearchair one grade lower, than the full expedition, which includes the second highest summit in the Torridon Mountains. Thus, while the optimum outing is described, the route has these easier options. 'Easy' is relative. No other path described in this book goes over a landscape so stripped to the naked bones of creation, no other hills offer such a shock of massive verticalities. This is a walk on the wild side.

ROUTE DESCRIPTION (Maps 23, 24)

The car-park lies on the north side of the road just west of the Allt Choire Dhuibhe Mhoir and the path sets off from between car-park and burn. A notice at the car-park points out the 'corrie of the hundred hills' across the glen on the lower slopes of Sgurr Dubh ('black peak'). These moraine deposits stand out clearest in the horizontal light of dawn or dusk and much of your day will be spent wandering through such 'lumpy' country *(1)*.

At first the path follows the stream, then heads more steeply up the hillside, so there is soon a bird's-eye view down onto the glen. Lochain an Iasgair below, is popular with fishermen. The square building by it is a boathouse; the trim cottage beyond is the Ling Hut *(2)*. Right of Sgurr Dubh the conical hill is Sgorr an Lochain Uaine ('peak of the green loch'). Both these are worthy Corbetts and behind them lie Beinn Liath Mor ('big grey hill') and Sgorr Ruadh ('red peak'), which are Munros.

The path rises continually (you do not realize by how much until descending it again) and slowly you are hemmed in by the great crags of Liathach's prow (L) and the screes and gullies of

STARTING POINT
Car-park, off A896 Kinlochewe-Torridon road. OS Outdoor Leisure Map 8 *The Cuillin and Torridon Hills* (958568).

FINISHING POINT
Car-park, off minor road from Torridon to Diabeg. OS Outdoor Leisure Map 8 *The Cuillin and Torridon Hills* (869576).

LENGTH
Glens only: 7½ miles (12 km). Including Coire Mhic Fhearchair: 10 miles (16 km). Including Ruadh-stac Mor: 12½ miles (20 km).

ASCENT
Glens only: 1020 ft (310 m). Including Coire Mhic Fhearchair: 1700 ft (520 m). Including Ruadh-stac Mor: 3050 ft (930 m).

mighty Beinn Eighe (R). Just before the path crosses the burn there is a boulder on the R which has neatly split in two. Stepping stones cross the burn. Another sprawling monster of a hill now fills the view ahead: Beinn Dearg ('red hill'), which falls short of Munro status by less than 3 ft (1 m) *(3)*.

The watershed is rather indefinite, but the path suddenly wends downwards noticeably. Soon after, an overgrown, crescent-shaped lochan lies to the R (the path crosses its tiny outflow) and, level with the far end, there is a cairn at a split in the path. Ignore the path heading off R and in 20 yards (18 m) two more cairns appear, marking the branching-off of another cairned route, R, which is the one to take for Coire Mhic Fhearchair. (The first fork also heads there but follows a rougher line and really only grew to prominence recently, beaten out by people coming out from Coire Mhic Fhearchair who had lost the original path.)

If you are just walking round behind Liathach, continue on the L options. After a brief rise the way ahead suddenly becomes visible. There is a bigger lochan, L, and its outflow curves away round under Beinn Dearg with several more lochans visible: this is the start of the Abhainn Coire Mhic Nobuil, which you follow down to the road. The path deteriorates badly as it is no longer an old 'made' path but merely one tramped out by passing walkers. Beware the black muddy bits!

Continuing on the (second) path R for Coire Mhic Fhearchair, the route weaves in and out and up and down the moraine deposits. A jutting crest suddenly gives a grand opening-up of the view and is a good spot for a pause *(4)*. Through the gap, R of Beinn Dearg, two more hills bulk large in the wilderness: Beinn en Eoin ('hill of the bird', a Corbett) and Beinn a' Chearcaill ('hill of the hoop'). Our path continues to curve round the flank of Sail Mhor, Beinn Eighe's westernmost peak, in a rhythm-destroying mix of boulders, bog and brae. There are plenty of alternatives but all (eventually) are squeezed upwards between the cleft north prow of Sail Mhor ('the big heel') and the tumbling waters draining the corrie of corries. When you reach the loch, cross the outflow and wander round the other side for the best view.

Quite a few claim this to be the most spectacular corrie in the country *(5)* for it is built round by natural battlements and even the view outwards is to a landscape pared to primitive ferocity.

Descend from the corrie by the route of ascent and take the lower path options to return to the jutting crest described

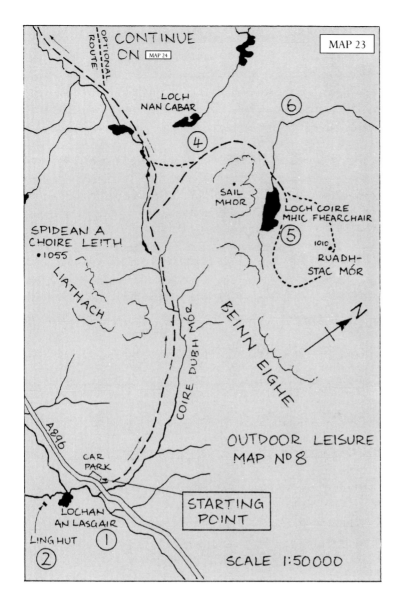

CONTINUE ON MAP 24

MAP 23

LOCH NAN CABAR

6

4

SAIL MHOR

LOCH COIRE MHIC FHEARCHAIR

SPIDEAN A CHOIRE LEITH
•1055

5

1010

RUADH-STAC MÓR

LIATHACH

COIRE DUBH MÓR

BEINN EIGHE

OUTDOOR LEISURE MAP N° 8

A896

CAR PARK

STARTING POINT

LOCHAN AN LASGAIR

LING HUT   1

2

SCALE 1:50000

OPTIONAL ROUTE

N

earlier, then head down (south-westwards) through the bumps
towards the end lochan (Loch Grobaig) where the Coire Mhic
Nobuil path is rejoined. Cutting the corner avoids the messy
reaches along by the lochans.

The ascent of Ruadh-stac Mor ('big red peak') is probably
enjoyed more in retrospect than during the ascent and descent,
for the hill is a disintegrating mess of unfriendly quartzite,
craggy or scree-girt and decidedly toilsome. Not for the timid or
unfit. In ascent I find it simplest just to head a bit north of east
and boldly ascend to the summit ridge, choosing a line with the
minimum of scree. The summit is just the highest point of an
elongated boulder plateau, which gives reasonable walking.
With only Liathach higher, the toil is rewarded by a big view.

Meall a' Ghiubhais ('yew tree hill') is another Corbett, as is Ruadh-stac Beag, Beinn Eighe's next jutting arm to the east. Beinn Eighe is, aptly, 'hill of the file'. The wild country beyond Loch Maree lies to the north-west, the loch itself glimpsed down Glen Grudie *(6)*.

From the summit of Ruadh-stac Mor head along and down to the neck which links the Munro to the main body of Beinn Eighe, and turn down into Coire Mhic Fhearchair by a rubbishy gully which is easier to descend than to climb. The ground, lower, is *very* broken and rough, with crags, boulders, bogs and streams galore. There is no set path: you 'dree your own weird' as we say. The east side of the loch is easier, but the more adventurous may choose to pass round between loch and Sail Mhor. Contour back and cut down as described above.

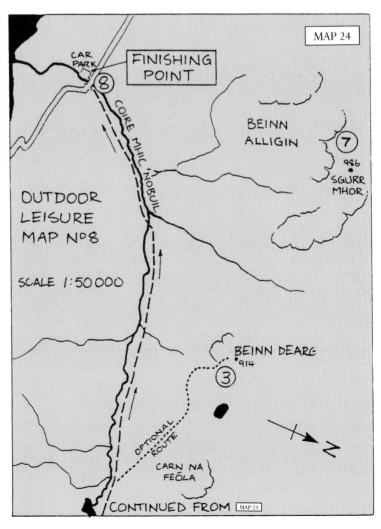

Liathach ('the grey one') with its great corries, towers and ragged crests, is seen at its wildest and best from this side: a mountaineer's mountain and one of the Top Ten in anybody's list of Scottish hills.

Liathach from above Shieldaig

The walk down Coire Mhic Nobuil is no anti-climax for, ahead, looms Beinn Alligin, the third of the giants of Torridon and, above, Beinn Dearg takes on an ever-grander aspect. (Unlike Lot's Wife, you are urged to look back, often.) The path does improve when it becomes old, 'made' path again and eventually merges with the one descending from the Bealach Chomhla to the north and, shortly after, crosses a footbridge at the confluence of rivers. An excellent path takes you down the L bank to the road.

The river now cuts down into a gorge and in several places diversions to look at waterfalls are recommended: there are obvious paths and you can probably *hear* the falls. There is a pleasant one below the footbridge leading to Alligin (7) and one not far from the road, and the last is seen by looking over the parapet of the bridge when the road is reached. The last bit of path runs through old Scots pines (8) and the road twisting down to Loch Torridon is much enhanced by this forest remnant. The last mile (1.6 km) also gives views over the loch to yet more Torridonian peaks.

1 Geology

These moraine deposits which litter all the Torridon glens are relatively new, in a geological timescale, being the result of the last Ice Age, almost 10,000 years ago, not long before man appeared on the scene. The Torridon Hills, on the other hand, date back to the dawn of the world, fabulously contorted and fashioned by unbelievable forces. Liathach can glow pink from its sandstone massiveness, yet is capped by quartzite which, across the glen, lies at valley level. Early geologists were puzzled. They just could not envisage hills stood on end! Sgurr Dubh across the valley is a *grey* hill, largely made of this Cambrian quartzite. Our path, initially, is made of this stone, then becomes the warmer, rufous colour as we gain the Torridon sandstone.

2 Ling Hut

The Ling Hut of the Scottish Mountaineering Club is named after one of the great unsung heroes of early British climbing, Willie Ling. He roamed Scotland all his life and took part in endless first ascents both at home and abroad (often with Harold Raeburn) in places such as Norway, the Alps and the Caucasus.

3 Beinn Dearg

The ascent of Beinn Dearg is an alternative to visiting Coire Mhic Fhearchair and Ruadh-stac Mor. You are looking more or less along the route of ascent from here: a long, easy-rising ascent to the ridge and then various towers to bypass (not altogether straightforward) to reach the summit. Return by the same route unless carrying a parachute.

4 Fossils

Some of the quartz boulders on this knoll have good examples of fossilized worm casts. Just 20 yards (18 m) before you reach the knoll a big slab actually lies on the path.

5 The Great Corrie

The division between sandstone and quartzite can plainly be seen on the cliffs, the two strata separated by Broad Terrace—named by a climber and with some understatement. From the lip of the corrie your voice echoes round it.

6 Nature Reserve

Most of the Beinn Eighe is part of a National Nature Reserve, with an important remnant of old forest along the shores of Loch Maree—a habitat favoured by pine-martens, while, anywhere today, the lucky walker could spot a lazy golden eagle soaring overhead.

7 *Great Cleft*

This waterfall has the Great Cleft of Alligin as background. This huge rift in the mountain, leading from just below the summit, right down into the corrie, is the result of a gigantic rockfall. The fallen rocks are spread across the moor below the cliffs—a fascinating spot to explore. It is known as 'the foxes' corrie'.

Liathach's western slopes above Loch Torridon

8 *Regeneration*

In the hills, overgrazing by sheep and deer prevents any natural regeneration of trees, so it is only in inaccessible gorges such as this, that trees have survived: birch, rowan and holly among them.

111

3·17

THE SUMMITS OF QUINAG

STARTING AND
FINISHING POINT
Car-park on the
east side of A894 on
Lairig Unapool.
(15-233274.)

LENGTH
8½ miles (14 km)

ASCENT
3940 ft (1200 m)

To drive from Ullapool to Unapool is to experience a sort of geological time warp. Startling hills crouch by the road like ambushing prehistoric monsters. Here are some of the oldest rocks in the world. In this skeleton of a place the protruding ribs of creation expose our puny human position of little and late. I have met people who have actually been frightened by the landscape of Coigach and Assynt. My own feelings never cease to be other than those of wonder—and surprise that a walker can venture into this vertical zoo relatively easily. Quinag, from most directions, looks as unapproachable as a panther but when you draw near you will hear the mountain purr.

ROUTE DESCRIPTION (Map 25)

Set off on the stalker's path almost opposite the car park, cross a burn and pull up for about ¼ mile (400 m) to gain a slight crest where you can swing L to gain the long westward-running ridge. It is well-defined with crags on its northern flank, and gives easy walking as the angle of ascent is the tilt of the quartzite strata which often breaks the surface, a surface which is completely littered with boulder debris. Despite the natural guidance of the edge, cairns have been erected. There is one rocky bump (15-212273), a small saddle, and then the final cone of the Corbett. The flat summit, from afar, looks like a well-defined castle but the main crags face north-east and one arrives quite unchallenged by difficulty. All the presumed difficulties will turn out to be imaginary but the setting is splendid and there is plenty of what climbers call 'exposure': the feeling of nothing below your boots! There is more green than expected and even if it is steep, there are few problems. When places are difficult they are obviously so.

The view is spread out as a grand panorama. Below is Loch Assynt and the big peaks of Inchnadamph backed by the Munros of Conival and Ben More; south is the grey Canisp and darker Suilven (1); east are Glas Bheinn and Beinn Leoid among a

112

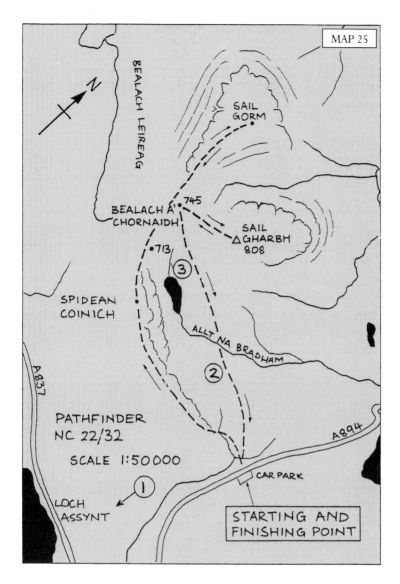

MAP 25

N

BEALACH LEIREAG

SAIL
GORM

•745
BEALACH A'
CHORNAIDH

SAIL
△GHARBH
808

•713

③

SPIDEAN
COINICH

ALLT NA BRADHAM

②

PATHFINDER
NC 22/32

A894

SCALE 1:50000

①

CAR PARK

LOCH
ASSYNT

STARTING AND
FINISHING POINT

A837

huddle of hills; north is the cone of Ben Stack and the mass of Arkle; while running right down the west is a frieze of coastline with the arabesques of the Outer Hebrides beyond the glitter of the Minch. Marvellous.

We head off to the north-west, dropping to a level crest and then up to a bump of 2340 ft (713 m). Keep looking back, for the Spidean profile certainly calls for photographs. A steep path now twists down to the Bealach a' Chornaidh. Pause on the descent to look into the eastern corrie, for this will be the line of descent *(2)*.

A path now heads up the other side of the col (a rock band is turned on the right) to the 2450 ft (745 m) Centre Top, which is really the hub of Quinag, from which spokes of ridge run out to the Corbetts. This is a good lunch spot and the day can

113

always be shortened by missing out Sail Gorm and going directly to Sail Gharbh, the highest summit of Quinag.

Descend the north-west ridge if you are aiming for Sail Gorm. There is one flat-topped rock-banded bump to traverse (a look-alike to Spidean's 'castle') before the lowest point, then some minor swellings, with cliffs to the west, before a steady pull up to the eyrie-like summit. The corrie on the right is Bathaich Cuinneige, 'the barn of Quinag', and it is possible to follow its stream down to the coastal road, but this is untracked and a very demanding alternative. Golden eagles and ravens frequent this quiet corner.

You traverse back, unavoidably, to the Centre Top, then east to the dip on the broad ridge running up to Sail Gharbh, which has the only Ordnance Survey obelisk of the day. Sail Gharbh is, strictly speaking, the thrust of cliffs that terminates the ridge but, for convenience, is used for the summit as well; the same applies to Sail Gorm.

From the dip to Centre Top it is quite possible to drop down, on grass, to pick up the stalkers' path—a descent studied earlier in the walk. The cairned path keeps over from the loch but on a sun-smiting day a swim off its warm-coloured sand spit will call for a diversion. (I've seen deer paddling in its waters!) The path should be regained before it crosses the Allt na Bradhan as the ground beyond is very bouldery: sandstone boulders dug up and pushed down the hill by glacial action—like a dog digging in slow motion! *(3)* The path makes a pleasant end to a memorable walk.

1 *Suilven*

This is a sort of Rock of Gibraltar set down in the Highlands. Norman McCaig, perhaps Scotland's finest living poet, has written many pieces about Suilven, his 'mountain of mountains'. Some are quoted in the anthologies *Speak to the Hills* and *Poems of the Scottish Hills* (Aberdeen University Press), and all appear in his *Collected Poems* (Chatto/Hogarth), one of the few such books to become a best-seller.

2 *Bealach a' Chornaidh path*

The path on which you began the walk does not end as shown on the map. It continues roughly on the same line to the Allt na Bradhan, crosses the burn, then arcs up into the head of the corrie, keeping well away from and then above Lochan Bealach Cornaidh. A steep path also drops west from the Bealach to the Gleann Leireag path linking Loch Assynt and the coastal road. From that side Quinag appears as a long

craggy ridge, gully-riven and scree-skirted.

Ardvreck Castle, Loch Assynt

Water is largely absent from the crests but a traverse from the Bealach a' Chornaidh will usually find a trickle or, if you are desperate, the burn descending to the lochan can be visited without too much of a re-ascent. In places it runs underground: audible but unobtainable!

3 Geology

Quinag is largely made of Torridonian sandstone, part of the band running from Applecross to Cape Wrath and including such great peaks as Liathach and An Teallach. Such was the earth's warping in the cataclysmic past that the underlying gneiss sometimes rises to some height—more than 1970 ft (600 m) on the prow of Sail Gorm. The highest cone of Quinag is actually a quartzite capping, a continuation of that so widely exposed on the ascent to Spidean Coinich and its 'castle'. Sail Gharbh's prow is of Torridonian sandstone, and as early as 1907, Raeburn, Ling and Mackay climbed its Barrel Buttress.

115

INTRODUCING THE CUILLIN OF SKYE

The Cuillin hills are unquestionably the wildest and most demanding range in Britain. Walkers often give the Cuillin a miss, believing them to be the preserve of the rock climber, but there are quite a few summits and passes which can be gained without technical difficulty. The following route, the Bealach a' Mhaim, is an ancient approach to remote Glenbrittle, having been used for centuries before the devious motor road was constructed. And with one of the easy Cuillin summits, Bruach na Frithe, lying above the pass, there is the bonus of a first scramble to the Cuillin crests. If you make that, then you are probably risking a lifetime of Cuillin exploration. If circumstances dictate a return to Sligachan (for the car, for instance) then reaching the pass and climbing Bruach na Frithe make for a grand day.

ACCESS
Buses run from Armdale and Kyleakin to Broadford and Portree, passing Sligachan, the start of the walk. If you drive to Glenbrittle, let one person drive round to the finish and the rest of the party can follow this traditional approach to the glen.

SAFETY NOTE
This route includes what is probably the roughest ascent described in the book, so walkers should be well-shod and carry good waterproofs and essential food. The pass could be forced in most conditions, but the ascent of Bruach na Frithe is best kept for a clear day as it may be a grade above your past walking experience. Furthermore, the compass is unreliable on top, the ordinary map is inadequate, and such a major ascent deserves the reward of the spectacular view – one of the best in Britain. Parts of the route can be wet and boggy and, on the hill itself, you are scrambling on bare rock. If you have traversed Crib Goch or Striding Edge then you may be relieved to know the traverse of Bruach na Frithe is no harder.

ROUTE DESCRIPTION (Maps 26, 27)

There are many paths heading off over the moors from Sligachan, so some care is needed at the start. Sligachan itself *(1)* is in a fine setting, with the pachydermatous hulk of Glamaig above *(2)*, a fine old pack bridge with a view up Glen Sligachan to Marsco *(3)*, and the jagged crests of the Sgurr nan Gillean-Am Bastier end of the Cuillin breaking over the horizon like a rush of black waves. The view has enthralled generations of walkers and climbers.

The A850 Kyleakin–Portree road has a branch, the A863, turning off at Sligachan, this latter road heading on to Dunvegan, with a road off the road reaching Glenbrittle. There is plenty of parking space at or near the hotel. A realigned bit of road behind the hotel, off the A863, is useful. Walk up the sweeping curve of the A863 and just beyond a shallow cutting a small road, roughly-tarred and with grass along the middle, heads L onto the moor. A small sign indicates 'Footpath to Glenbrittle' and two lines of power and telephone poles also head off onto the moor. There is a small roadside car-park. Other tracks between the hotel and here should be ignored.

Follow this minor road. Its reason soon becomes obvious: road and posts head to a lonely, white building: Alltdearg House. At the gate pillar of its fenced-off grounds, turn R (an arrow is painted on the post) for a squelchy diversion before rejoining the old made path *(4)*.

The going is actually not too bad as the path winds up along beside the waters of the Allt Dearg Mor, a quite delightful burn with seemingly countless cascades and tempting pools. The jagged towers of Sgurr nan Gillean's Pinnacle Ridge stand out finely from the path with the blunt upthrust of Am Basteir and the battle-axe of the Basteir Tooth.

The Allt Dearg Mor gathers most of its waters in Coire na Circe, from which the path climbs up towards the Bealach a' Mhaim. As you look south, the big Fionn Choire is clear* (see overleaf). A spring, Tobar nan Uaislean (5) lies by the path on the last stretch to the pass (6).

There is a pool on the watershed, marking the start of the Allt a' Mhaim. Then there is a proper lochan, beyond which a side path breaks off L to circle the head of Coire na Creiche, giving access to various climbs and a tricky pass to Coruisk. Continue on past a big cairn for the descent down into Glenbrittle. The size of the cairn is an indication of the long use of this pass. The path angles down for ⅝ mile (1 km) to the corner of the huge forestry plantations which you skirt until you reach the motor road to Glenbrittle.

There is a good view into Coire na Creiche, a huge empty bowl drained by the River Brittle, another river with many

117

waterfalls (7). The other side of the corrie is dominated by the prow of Sgurr Thuilm and jutting out from the back of the corrie is the split triangular peak of Sgurr an Fheadain.

From the point where you reach the road it is 2¼ miles (3.5 km) to the hostel, 2¾ miles (4.5 km) to the hut and other houses, and 3½ miles (5.5 km) to the campsite. If being met by a car, the bridge over the River Brittle, ⅝ mile (1 km) down the valley, is a good rendezvous (8-416245).

1 *Sligachan*

The historic inn here was the base for much of the early exploration of the Cuillin. The visitors' book dating back to

*If you are heading for Bruach na Frithe, simply break off the main path to head up into the corrie.

BRUACH NA FRITHE

There are a variety of routes, so you can choose your own combination of ascent and descent lines.

ASCENT 1

A cairned path breaks off the main path from Coire na Circe and heads up west of the Allt an Fhionn-Choire to gain the ridge that demarcates the corrie on its west side. Once the crest of this North-west Ridge is gained it is just a matter of picking a line along and up it to the summit. In places there is some scrambling but any trickier places can be bypassed on the R and L flanks. Keep to the crest as much as possible or you may traverse off onto real crags. Climbers would regard this as an easy ridge but walkers who normally amble hands-in-pockets will find it a novel excitement. (9).

ASCENT 2

The completely easy way is simply to wander up the Fionn Choire, a surprisingly green and flowery place as the surface is somewhat porous (even the streams vanish in places), to reach the scree-covered slopes at the head of the corrie. Climb up to the lowest point on the ridge and ascend the easy East Ridge. Bruach na Frithe is topped by the Main Ridge's only Ordnance Survey obelisk. Most of this route is cairned or well-worn in the upper parts.

ALTERNATIVE DESCENTS

The East Ridge and Fionn Choire provide the easiest way down from Bruach na Frithe, but the North-west Ridge is the most entertaining and can be followed all the way down to the saddle of the Bealach a' Mhaim. Heed the warnings about navigational problems in cloud – and keep this hill for a clear day. All running water from the Fionn Choire ends at Sligachan, so you should be mislaid rather than lost.

those days has, alas, been stolen and something of the *The classic view to the* atmosphere has gone as busloads of trippers swarm around in *Cuillin from Sligachan* the summer. It was to the inn that the great Norman Collie retired in the lonely war years. Richard Hillary in his classic story of his flying days, *The Last-Enemy*, paints a picture of Collie, and their own escapade on the Sligachan hills. C. Mill's *Norman Collie, A Life in Two Worlds* (Aberdeen University Press) is a recent biography I can recommend.

2 *Glamaig*

This brutal Corbett was the scene of an early escapade which still offers a feat hard to emulate. In 1899 one of General Bruce's Gurkhas romped up and down Glamaig, in bare feet, in just 55 minutes. In 1955 George Rhodes took a couple of minutes longer, but I have not read of any improvement on the time.

3 *Marsco*

This is the hill that dominates the view up Glen Sligachan even if it does not make Corbett height. A traverse from Glamaig to Marsco is one of Skye's great walks as it gives an endless view to the Black Cuillin. These hills are Red Cuillin and largely composed of crumbling red granite screes, so careful route-finding is called for. Glen Sligachan offers a long walk through to Loch Scavaig or Elgol. One renowned hiker through Glen Sligachan was Bonnie Prince Charlie during his wanderings after Culloden. Obviously conditions have changed little. An old lady, dealing with his feet after the walk, commented 'Filthy lad!'

4 *Weather*

To be fair, a warning should be given about Skye's weather.

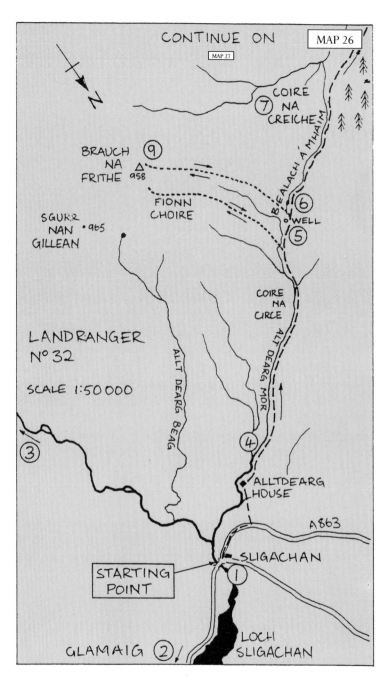

The siting of such big hills in the west ensures that they receive a large share of our moist westerly weather. Wet here can be very wet indeed and in prolonged rain one should simply flee, and come again. There is a tremendous run-off of water and in a heatwave the Cuillin can be surprisingly waterless. The moors round the hills, often lying on impervious rock, act as sponges and the paths across them have become black morasses.

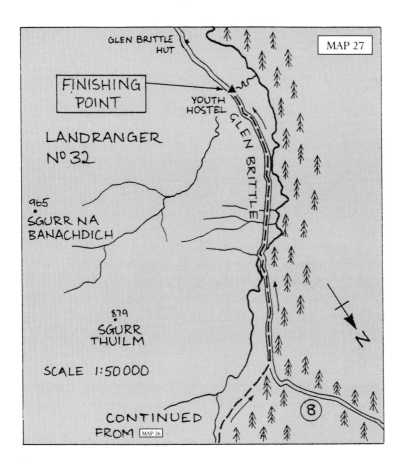

MAP 27

GLEN BRITTLE HUT

FINISHING POINT

YOUTH HOSTEL

GLEN BRITTLE

LANDRANGER Nº 32

965
SGURR NA BANACHDICH

879
SGURR THUILM

SCALE 1:50 000

CONTINUED FROM MAP 26

8

5 *Tobar nan Uaislean*

'The well of the gentlemen' is a well in the Scottish sense; that is, a spring. It lies just below the path a couple of minutes short of the watershed.

6 *The Bealach a' Mhaim*

'The pass of the rounded hill' is usually just called the Mam ('the saddle'), which is what it is rather than a defile. If you are not contemplating the ascent of Bruach na Frithe, then wander up onto Am Ban above, to enjoy the panoramic view, which is obscured in the pass itself.

7 *Coire na Creiche*

This is 'the corrie of the spoils', 'spoils' referring to rustled cattle. No doubt animals driven over the Bealach a' Mhaim were secreted here successfully. No road entered the glen in those days. A vicious clan battle here saw the MacDonalds defeat the MacLeods in 1601, a fray which much embarrassed James VI, who was trying to impress Queen Elizabeth I of England with his control of Scotland.

The Cuillin was once the centre of violent volcanic activity. A slow-cooking lava formed the rough, dark gabbro rock we all love. Basalt intrusions have eroded more rapidly

and have created the gullies and chimneys which are so characteristic. Waterpipe Gully, down Sgurr an Fheadain, is typical. Finally, it was the scouring glaciers that dug out the corries and left the narrow crests. The geology of Skye is very much open to the eye.

Coire na Creiche is one of only five sites (all in Skye) where the alpine rock cress *Arabis alpina* grows in Britain. The gabbro does not produce an exciting flora but you will meet all the alpine regulars. And in a few places there are special plants like the above.

8 *The road to Glenbrittle*

About 5 miles (8 km) from Sligachan you leave the Dunvegan road to take a side road for Carbost and 1¼ miles (2 km) later this is in turn left for a narrow road over desolate moors. There are grand views of the Cuillin as the road dips through the plantings.

9 *Bruach na Frithe*

Bruach na Frithe (pronounced *Broo-ach na Free*), 'slope of the deer forest', is 3143 ft (958 m) and will probably have taken 3–4 hours to scale, from Sligachan. The first recorded ascent was made in May 1845 by Professor Forbes, the early glaciologist, who dutifully took his barometer to the top.

Beyond the jagged crest over Am Basteir looms Sgurr nan Gillean (3166 ft, 965 m), 'the peak of the young men'. At Bruach na Frithe the Main Ridge turns sharply southwards over the least-visited lower section before the complex peaks of Sgurr a' Mhadaidh and Sgurr a' Ghreadaidh lead on to the most popular area above Glenbrittle. This area includes Sgurr Alasdair (3257 ft, 993 m), Skye's highest peak, the Inaccessible Pinnacle, the most difficult of all Munros, and Sgurr na Banachdich, the only other walkers' Munro in the Cuillin. A traverse of the whole ridge is still regarded as one of the greatest days possible on our hills.

APPENDICES

ACCESS

It is frequently said that there is no law of trespass in Scotland, but that statement is erroneous. The modern situation is that walkers and climbers have a factual freedom-to-roam in wild places provided there is consideration for estate needs, and that countryside sensibilities operate.

It is because of this *de facto* situation that there is widespread public misunderstanding about the *de jure* position. The law says that a landowner has the right to request a walker to leave his land, and may possibly exert just sufficient force to achieve that object; a situation fraught with the possibility of counter-charges, and which rarely happens and which, in many cases in Scotland, would not be obeyed. The mere fact of being on the ground in Scotland is not, *of itself*, an offence and legal actions over access are a matter of the civil, not the criminal, law.

Such actions over access are virtually unheard of, and most Scottish walkers passionately believe they have a *moral* right to wander in wild places and will not surrender it. However, such an attitude should be accompanied by a knowledge of estate and farming needs. In outlining the legal position, one must emphasize that the main feature of walker-landowner relationships in Scotland is one of cordial co-existence on a voluntary basis.

Traditional freedom to roam in Scotland was greatly changed by nineteenth-century legislation that resulted from the creation of the big sporting estates, and which enabled owners to take prohibitive legal action against people walking on their ground. Some routes were obviously needed for community purposes such as droving, funerals, ways to markets, or passage between settled communities, and corridor rights-of-way were then defined which had the protection of the law and which still exist as legal, free-access routes. There were some spectacular court cases before these routes were clarified.

As the years passed and the social pattern of ownership of hill areas changed, and as more and more people went to the outdoors, this situation eased. Men who took part in two world wars were in no mood for restrictions on walking when they returned. And as the outdoor boom developed, a *de facto* freedom-to-roam evolved.

A landowner can still take legal, civil action against a walker to prevent him entering or re-entering the ground, but normally has to prove damage or harm before such a ban would be granted by the court. As no damage is normally caused by walking hills, glens and moors, examples of such litigation are very few.

Tresspass legislation means the police can be involved if fires are lit without permission or camping is carried out without permission. This legislation was originally brought in to deal with the travelling people, the tinkers, camping on sites against the wishes of the owner. It has been used against hillwalkers in modern times in some isolated instances.

Scotland now has a situation whereby most landowners recognize the desire of people to walk and make no attempt to prevent it, but understandably seek co-operation over deer stalking dates and at some other key times. Most walkers believe freedom to roam in the hills to be a moral right and will not surrender it, but want to cause no bother. Privacy, crops, farm stock and agricultural needs must be respected. Reservoirs and park land are covered by regulations. The extent and range of relatively wild land in Scotland and a small population of five million help this situation to work although there are some localized pressure-points.

Modern factors which can affect freedom to roam include the growth of private forestry plantations, which can blanket some access glens or paths, the Ministry of Defence closing certain areas; or new owners who do not understand Scottish traditions; or the behaviour of some cavalier walkers.

DOGS

Where there are sheep around, dogs are best kept on a leash. They can be shot on sight if a shepherd has reasonable grounds for thinking sheep have been chased or frightened. Dogs should be under control at all times.

GATES

They must be shut after you unless they are already open when you get there, in which case they should be left open.

SHEEP

When sheep have lambs give them a wide berth in case you disturb ewes with sick young ones. If a lamb follows you, ignore it. If you see a shepherd or dogs driving sheep near you, get out of the way or sit still until they have passed.

LITTER

All litter should be taken home. Some countryside litter bins are anything but effective. They often have no lids, so scavengers spread the rubbish around and the wind scatters the top layers of paper and plastic.

GROUSE

The season starts on 12 August and has its peak during that month. It ends on 10 December. Such areas are easily recognized by the presence of shooting butts, small palisades or bunkers of stone, turf, wood or corrugated iron. Stay clear in season.

RED DEER

The stag shooting season runs from 1 July to 20 October, and that for hinds from 21 October to 15 February. In practice, the main time is mid-August to round mid-October. Few estates request walkers to stay off the hills from July to February and those who do are a bone of contention. Consult locally during the peak period or go to non-shooting hills. The balance between consultation on a route during shooting times and asking permission is a fine one, but the line should be recognized. Shooting is not traditionally carried out on a Sunday, but there are some modern exceptions to this and walkers can move the deer on a Sunday to the detriment of an estate plan for the Monday. The letting of shooting rights or the sale of venison form a major part of the income of many estates.

In outlining the legal position and countryside behaviour in Scotland, one must make it clear that the overall position is currently a relatively happy one. A series of legal actions would end current co-existence and could not be made to stick, and landowners would be the ultimate losers. Uncaring and irresponsible individual climbers and walkers can do untold harm. No one wants friction and that is how it should be. Freedom-to-roam is a precious heritage, but it brings responsibilities for caring behaviour with it and many walkers are glad to number estate owners, factors, shepherds and stalkers among their close friends, and vice versa.

Scottish Natural Heritage, the Government's environmental advisory board in Scotland, is currently undertaking a national review of the access position.

SAFETY

The wilderness and remoteness of parts of Scotland, especially the Highlands, cannot be emphasized too strongly. For those used to walking in England, there is an altogether different, harder challenge, both mentally and physically. In the Lake District, for example, you are seldom more than a few miles from a road – and Lakeland is much smaller. In the Highlands, however, there are some sheets of the 1:50 000 map with only a few inches of red road marked on them. The walking game is a far more serious one in the north.

Even some of the easy walks can be hazardous at times. You should think twice before a Caithness clifftop walk when a gale is raging through the Pentland Firth, and parts of the Borders can be very remote from any help in an emergency. The rather parrot-fashion rules need to be supplanted by a single, vital imperative: THINK. The hills can get round the rules, having plenty of original dirty tricks for the unwary but, whatever the circumstances, there is always a best action/reaction. Don't panic. Think the situation through and do your best. A few basic guidelines may help.

Go well equipped. An efficient waterproof, windproof 'shell' and adequate warm layers underneath should be the norm. A 'bivvy' bag should be carried.

Make sure you have map and compass, and know how to use them. All the party should be able to navigate, not just the leader.

If going alone, leave some indication of your plans. Walking alone is a valid mountain game, not lightly undertaken however, and best learnt on easy terrain. The harder walks in this book are only suitable for the experienced solo walker.

Be prepared to modify routes when weather or circumstances dictate; as many accidents are caused by sticking to a set plan as by neglecting one. The hills have the last say, not us.

Carry useful foods, and some extra. The calories will be burnt up at a great rate and need to be replaced: little and often is sound advice. Take in plenty of liquid. A group can carry a pan and stove and enjoy brewing-up. You watch your car's fuel gauge, so watch your own consumption.

Keep an eye on the weather. Ask local advice or make use of TV or radio forecasts. Obtain, and use, a Met Office card listing telephone numbers for area forecasts.

Carry a basic first aid kit. Deal with any rubbing on heels at once; blisters not only cripple, they cause delays and benightments. Learn some first aid; it could save a life. If there is an accident, keep calm. Render such first aid as you can and shelter the patient. Write down a six-figure grid reference and a note of the injuries. *Then* head out for help. The nearest telephone may be nearly a day's walk away, remember. Dial 999 and pass on the information to the police, who organize rescue services in Scotland.

Be comfortable in your walking. Wear appropriate clothing and footwear for the weather and conditions. Take off and put on garments as required. Often the summit is not the best place to rest. Find better shelter and keep warm. Conversely, avoid overheating. Heat exhaustion is not uncommon. Wearing waterproofs in a heatwave is not a good idea, but it is seen and, in one case, heat exhaustion was put down to hypothermia because the symptoms seem the same. There is no substitute for thinking, so

THINK

THINK

THINK.

GIVING A GRID REFERENCE

Giving a grid reference is an excellent way of 'pinpointing' a feature, such as a church or mountain summit, on an Ordnance Survey map.

Grid lines, which are used for this purpose, are shown on the 1:25 000 Outdoor Leisure, 1:25 000 Pathfinder and 1:50 000 Landranger maps produced by the Ordnance Survey; these are the maps most commonly used by walkers. Grid lines are the thin blue lines one kilometre apart going vertically and horizontally across the map producing a network of small squares. Each line, whether vertical or horizontal, is given a number from 00 to 99, with the sequence repeating itself every 100 lines. The 00 lines are slightly thicker than the others thus producing large squares each side representing 100 km and made up of 100 small squares. Each of these large squares is identified by two letters. The entire network of lines covering the British Isles, excluding Ireland, is called the National Grid.

FIGURE 3 Giving a grid reference

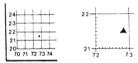

The left-hand diagram above shows a corner of an Ordnance Survey 1:50 000 Landranger map which contains a Youth Hostel. Using this map, the method of determining a grid reference is as follows:

Step 1

Holding the map in the normal upright position, note the number of the 'vertical' grid line to the left of the hostel. This is 72.

Step 2

Now imagine that the space between this grid line and the adjacent one to the right of the hostel is divided into ten equal divisions (the right-hand diagram does this for you). Estimate the number of these 'tenths' that the hostel lies to the right of the left-hand grid line. This is 8. Add this to the number found in Step 1 to make 728.

Step 3

Note the number of the grid line below the hostel and add it on to the number obtained above. This is 21, so that the number becomes 72821.

Step 4

Repeat Step 2 for the space containing the hostel, but now in a vertical direction. The final number to be added is 5, making 728215. This is called a six-figure grid reference. This, coupled with the number or name of the appropriate Landranger or Outdoor Leisure map, will enable the Youth Hostel to be found.

A full grid reference will also include the identification of the appropriate 100 kilometre square of the National Grid; for example, SD 728215. This information is given in the margin of each map.

ADDRESSES OF USEFUL ORGANIZATIONS

Association for the Protection
of Rural Scotland,
Gladstone's Land,
483 Lawnmarket,
Edinburgh, EH1 2NT.
Edinburgh (031) 225 7913

Forestry Commission,
Public Information Division,
231 Corstorphine Road,
Edinburgh, EH12 7AT.
Edinburgh (031) 334 0303

National Trust for Scotland,
5 Charlotte Square,
Edinburgh, EH2 4DU.
Edinburgh (031) 226 5922

Scottish Conservation Projects
Trust,
Balallan House,
24 Allan Park,
Stirling, FK8 2QG.
Stirling (0786) 479 697

Scottish Countryside Rangers
Association,
PO Box 37,
Stirling, SK8 2BL.

Scottish Inland Waterways
Association,
139 Old Dalkeith Road,
Edinburgh, EH16 4SZ.
Edinburgh (031) 664 1070

Scottish Natural Heritage,
12 Hope Terrace,
Edinburgh, EH9 2AS.
Edinburgh (031) 447 4784

Scottish Natural Heritage,
(South-east region),
Battleby,
Redgorton,
Perth, PH1 3EW.
Perth (0738) 27921

Scottish Rights of Way Society,
10 Sunnyside,
Edinburgh, EH7 5RA.
Edinburgh (031) 652 2937

Scottish Tourist Board,
23 Ravelston Terrace
Edinburgh, EH4 3EU.
Edinburgh (031) 332 2433

Scottish Youth Hostels
Association,
7 Glebe Crescent,
Stirling, FK8 2JA.
Stirling (0786) 451 181

Scottish Wildlife Trust,
Cramond House,
Kirk Cramond,
Cramond Glebe Road,
Edinburgh, EH4 6NS.
Edinburgh (031) 312 7765

INDEX